CONFIDENTIAL

Also by Joan Bolker, Ed.D.

*The Writer's Home Companion:
An Anthology of the
World's Best Writing Advice,
from Keats to Kunitz*

Writing Your Dissertation in Fifteen Minutes a Day

JOAN BOLKER, Ed.D.

Writing Your Dissertation in Fifteen Minutes a Day

· · · · · · · ·

A GUIDE TO STARTING,

REVISING, AND FINISHING

YOUR DOCTORAL THESIS

A HOLT PAPERBACK

Henry Holt and Company · New York

Holt Paperbacks
Henry Holt and Company, LLC
Publishers since 1866
175 Fifth Avenue
New York, New York 10010
www.henryholt.com

Library of Congress Cataloging-in-Publication Data
Bolker, Joan.
Writing your dissertation in fifteen minutes a day :
a guide to starting, revising, and finishing your doctoral thesis /
Joan Bolker. — 1st ed.
p.   cm.
Includes bibliographical references (p.   ) and index.
ISBN-13: 978-0-8050-4891-9
ISBN-10: 0-8050-4891-X
1. Dissertations, Academic—Authorship.   2. Report writing.
3. Academic writing.   I. Title.
LB2369.B57   1998
808'.066378—dc21   98-5262

Henry Holt books are available for special promotions and
premiums. For details contact: Director, Special Markets.

First Holt Paperbacks Edition 1998

Designed by Victoria Hartman

Printed in the United States of America

21   23   22

For EDB

—*Placet*

Contents

~

Acknowledgments

MANY PEOPLE have contributed to the making of this book
with support of many kinds: with practical help, suggestions of
topics and ideas, their own words, editing, and teaching. I want
to thank first the many graduate students who have worked on
(and for the most part completed) their dissertations in my presence and taught me what was and wasn't helpful to them.

I am grateful to Irene Fairley and Carl Steinitz, not only for their
interest in and support of this project, but also for suggesting and
contributing to the appendix chapter on advice for advisors; Carl
Steinitz also allowed me to include his description of how he
writes; Rob Socolow made several helpful suggestions for that
same chapter. Thanks to Susan Gubar and John Burt for good talk
about graduate students and their struggles; Bob Kiely, for permitting me to tell the story of his dissertation; William Alfred, Peter
Elbow, Albert Guerard, Kiyo Morimoto, William G. Perry Jr., and
Ruth Whitman, for showing me much of what I know about first-
rate teaching and writing; Jane Prager, for listening closely; Robin
Straus, Theresa Burns, and Amy Rosenthal, for starting this book
on its way; Maggie Carr, for careful and sensitive copyediting of

the book; Robin Straus and Tracy Sherrod, for invaluable help in bringing it to completion; Susan Lorand, for fine editorial help; Peg Frank, Bonnie Glaser, Connie Lewis, Ellen Marks, Patsy Sharaf, and Anita Shishmanian, for their ongoing support; Pat and Margaret Kilcoyne, for Latin consultations and many other things; Anne-Marie Smith, for allowing me the privilege of watching her grow as a writer over half of her life so far, and for cheering my writing efforts.

Thanks to my daughter, Jessica Bolker, for her many suggestions and superb editorial help, and for the benefit of her thoughtful experience as a graduate student in zoology, which is woven into the fabric of this book; to my son, Ben Bolker, who edited, asked the right questions, contributed extensively to the appendix chapter on computers, and talked with me willingly, and at a moment's notice, about both technical issues and the particular concerns of doctoral students in the sciences; and to Peter Bixby, who shared the process of his thesis writing with me, even in medias res, allowed me to use his description of his revising process, and meticulously edited the early chapters of this book.

Thanks to Vicky Steinitz, my own thesis advisor, who showed me how it was done at its best.

And finally, to Ethan Bolker—the list is too long even to enumerate.

Introduction

FOR OVER THIRTY YEARS I've listened to writers as they've talked about their work. The hundreds of doctoral students among them who've consulted me in order to finish their dissertations have taught me how to help others to give themselves good writing advice. This book is a collection of successful field-tested strategies for writing a dissertation; it's also a guide to conducting an experiment, with you as your own subject, your work habits as the data, and a writing method that fits you well as the goal. *Writing Your Dissertation* is for two audiences: its primary audience is the graduate student who is either about to begin or has already begun writing a dissertation, but thesis advisors will find it useful, too.

I've worked hard on two dissertations of my own. The first was on medieval literature. It occupied me for four or five years, and I never completed it. I quit that Ph.D. program shortly after my committee had accepted my first chapter. I began writing my second dissertation, a study of the intersection of individual psychological development, curriculum development, and writing competence, about four years later and finished it in a few months. Clearly I'd learned something in between. I've learned more since. My own experiences as a writer, and what others have told me about what works for them (dividing up large tasks, setting themselves short-term deadlines) and what doesn't (writing binges, trying to write after a full day's work) are distilled in this book so that you can learn from our struggles.

This is not just a writing book. It doesn't simply focus on the limited task of transcribing your research results into the required format. When I speak about "writing your dissertation," I mean the entire event, from the first stirrings you note in yourself of a deep interest in a field, a research problem, or a theme, through the iterations of possible ideas, to a finished manuscript. Under the rubric of "writing" I include your research, the first hesitantly scribbled notes to yourself, the zero draft, the first draft, drafts that follow, and the final one, as well as the thesis defense and the transformation of your dissertation into published articles or a book.

You might ask, "Why focus on the writing of a dissertation when the major problem is doing the research?" Because to do research is to inquire, to dig one's way into a problem, and writing is one of the best tools available for such work. I will show you how to use writing to think, to explore, to blunder, to question yourself, to express frustration, to question further, to get to what feels like the truth of your subject. And to celebrate.

The writing process is inherently complicated. We can tell by the number of shelves given over to books about it in libraries (including my own). What is different about this book, that justifies adding it to those already overfilled shelves? Most writing texts give you specific advice based on the assumption that writers are either all like the author or all like each other. I've worked with enough students (a few thousand, I'd guess) in enough different settings to know that people learn (and don't learn) and educate themselves in many different ways and styles. There is no single writing method that will suit even most of the people most of the time. There is, though, a way of looking at the writing process that gets at its heart and allows you to imagine how you want to interact with it. I am not proposing a single strategy for writing; I want to teach you to find *the process that works best for you*. This book is as much about learning to develop such a process as it is about writing.

Writing Your Dissertation will be full of suggestions for ways to improve your writing process, to make it more efficient, and more likely to produce a piece of work that's less likely to kill you in its making, a piece you'll be proud of. If you already have some strategy that serves you well, it doesn't matter how bizarre it is: you can write in toothpaste, or in a closet, and if it produces good writing in a reasonable length of time without harming you, then use it. (But be sure to ask yourself if it really works, or if you love it just because you've been using it for ten years.) Use the techniques I describe to invent your own strategies.

I won't talk about rules that you should either follow or break. There are no rules in this book. There are some principles, stances to be explored, ways to imagine what to experiment with. Try applying them, and see how they work with your own ways of writing. If you don't like what happens, if the principles feel not quite right, or inefficient, or they get in your way, then adapt the advice in this book or scrap it and invent your own. The particular suggestions I've made are fashioned of clay, not stone.

Throughout *Writing Your Dissertation* I will speak about ownership of writing. One of my fundamental assumptions is that writers own their writing. Many things follow from this

assumption: most important is that you have the largest investment in the outcome of your project, so you are the only person
responsible for carrying it forward. I've had numerous experiences that suggest many students and advisors don't see dissertation work this way. Since a basic premise of this book is that the
writing process is an ongoing experiment, it follows that you are
in charge of that experiment, that you can shape your writing
into what you want it to be, using a method that suits your personality and work style.

I've found some surprising agreements about writing among
theorists of very different stripes: Peter Elbow, the author of
Writing Without Teachers (a radical text when it was first published in 1973), and B. F. Skinner, known for his invention/dis-
covery of behavioral psychology, both believe in *writing in order
to think*, rather than *thinking in order to write*. Given their philo-
sophical differences, it's a fair bet that we're looking at the truth,
and you'll want to consider how to incorporate it into your own
writing process.

You might wonder about the usefulness of a general book on
how to write a dissertation, given that every field has its own
requirements for a dissertation's shape and content. At first
glance, theses in science and the humanities would seem to
require different processes. But my experience with writers in
each area has shown me that this first glance is misleading, and
that there are, in fact, far more similarities between the two than
one might expect. Certainly the external contexts in which
these dissertations are written are different. Potential science
Ph.D.'s are more likely to move along smoothly when they are
actually writing. One reason may be that they often get substantial financial support for their projects; some of their speediness
may come from their having been given research problems by

their advisors, and having solved them by the time they actually sit down to write. It is much more obvious that the humanities thesis writer is engaged in telling a story, that there is a gradually unfolding narrative of ideas that are shown finally to be linked to each other, a narrative that comes into existence as it is being written. But although it's easier to pretend in science that one first "does it" and then "writes it up," this idea greatly oversimplifies the way in which scientific inquiry really happens. In science, as in other fields, discovering the holes in your theories and arguments as you write helps you produce better and more creative science. As C. P. Snow told us eloquently years ago, the inquiry of science is also a narrative process, the telling of a story, so the young science dissertation writer is well served if she tends to that narrative aspect from the beginning of her inquiry. The writing of a doctoral thesis turns out to be a more universal process than is immediately obvious.

Although I'm a psychologist by profession, this book is not about do-it-yourself therapy. Even if it were possible to do your own therapy (which strikes me as on a par with taking out your own appendix), there are usually more efficient modes than psychoanalysis to help you finish your dissertation. *Writing Your Dissertation* is based on some useful and easily learned behavioral principles, such as "Negative reinforcement is not very useful for encouraging behavior; positive reinforcement works much better." One of the most common mistakes struggling thesis writers make is self-flagellation; it impedes their progress. My hope is that this book will help you substitute the carrot for the stick.

I've given this book the title *Writing Your Dissertation in Fifteen Minutes a Day* because I thought it would get your attention; but it's also true that if you begin by working on your thesis fifteen minutes every day, you will dramatically increase the odds that you'll finish it. So one of the most important pieces of advice in this book is, *Do some work on your thesis every day, even if it's only for fifteen minutes.* ("Every day" is more important than how much time you spend, or how many pages you produce, or what quality of work you produce on any particular day.) Although I've known people who have produced finished theses in wildly varying lengths of time, anywhere from six weeks to ten years, I don't actually know anyone who's done it in only fifteen minutes a day. But I do know many who began the process that led them to complete their dissertations by writing for only a very short time every day.

Writing Your Dissertation is arranged to parallel the dissertation process itself: The first four chapters discuss the tasks and attitudes you need to consider as you get started on your project. Some of them—like the selection of an advisor—may take place before you have put even a single word on paper or disk. The next three chapters are about the middle part of the process—the actual writing—about what to do if you get stuck, and how other people are involved in the project. (In particular, chapter 6 discusses how to deal with those interruptions, generated either by the outside world or by your own insides, that intrude on your thesis work.) The chapters that follow are about those times, both exhilarating and sad, when the end of your dissertation is in sight and you begin to turn your attention to life after it. Chapter 8 talks about revising from the first draft through to the final one. Chapter 9 addresses the various complex events, from psychological crises to your thesis defense, that take place at the end of the dissertation-writing process. Chapter 10 focuses on your life after you've been awarded your doctorate, and on whether or not to publish your dissertation or to continue a writing life. The first appendix considers the applications of the computer revolution to dissertation writing; the second is written particularly for your advisor.

I hope you will find *Writing Your Dissertation* good company as you begin the adventure of writing a dissertation. My daughter put off starting her thesis for a month, saying she had a conference paper that needed finishing, but knowing what her real reason was: she had heard so many horror stories about dissertation writing from other people that she wasn't eager to begin a long period of her life that she expected would be miserable. She tells me that, to her surprise, most of the process turned out to be a pleasure for her, and she wishes someone had told her in advance that this was possible. So I'll let her tell you: writing a dissertation can be a pleasure, at least some of the time. And even if it doesn't turn out to be for you, the advice in this book can still help you write a fine thesis.

Writing Your Dissertation is a do-it-yourself book. Make it your own, leave behind the pieces that don't work for you, rewrite it so it suits your own particular learning style, and use it in ways that will support your progress. Some writers really do enjoy writing their dissertations. This book is meant to help you become one of those writers.

*Writing Your Dissertation
in Fifteen Minutes a Day*

1

Beginning

IF YOU ENJOY RESEARCH and writing, some of the greatest gifts life can offer you are time, space, and a good rationalization for devoting yourself to a project that truly interests you. But there are many other stances from which to approach writing a doctoral dissertation. Most of the students I meet in my work don't often think of their dissertation projects with joyful anticipation. Instead, they're overwhelmed by the size of the task, or they don't consider themselves scholars, or they are scared that they're not up to it, or they don't even know how to begin. But even if you're not a true scholar yet (whatever that is) or are feeling frightened, you can still write a good dissertation, using a process that minimizes pain and increases your chances of feeling engaged and satisfied with your work. And the first step is to imagine your dissertation.

The best way to begin a dissertation is not by positioning yourself in a library and writing "Chapter 1" on the top of a blank piece of paper. The best way to begin is by approaching your dissertation in your imagination, preparing to write in and about this thesis at every stage, and to become the researcher of your own work process. Imagining your dissertation allows you to develop passion, curiosity, and questions about your topic, as well as to think of yourself as someone who can make a commitment to scholarship. You may be given a topic. You may be so terrified you can't imagine "passion" or "pleasure" as words with any relevance to your undertaking. You may be writing a thesis for strictly instrumental reasons. Nevertheless, it's still worth imagining—choosing and playing with different topics and different types of theses, giving yourself some leeway to explore before you commit to a particular topic in a specific format. You can take time at this point to speculate about how it will feel to have done this work, to own a doctorate. Or you can think about the process by which you hope to research and write, and where you'll try to do your writing. You can imagine how much company you'd like or will need—friends, coworkers, the active presence of your committee—during this project, and whom you'll ask to be your advisor and your committee members. You may even want to consider seriously how you would feel, what might happen, if you were to choose not to write a dissertation.

People write dissertations for many different reasons. For some of you the goal is to meet a professional necessity, to accomplish an instrumental task: you want to spend your professional life teaching at a college or university, and you know that a doctorate is a prerequisite. Others want to learn the process of producing a major scholarly work, to begin a life of serious research and writing. Still others, before they go on to the next phase of life, want to finish a process they began some time back when they entered graduate school. And then there are the lucky ones who have a burning question that they want to spend time answering. One of the ways to begin, no matter which of these agendas is yours, is by learning to write your way in.

Writing Your Way In

Writing is at the center of producing a dissertation. This book will teach you how not to talk away your ideas or lose them in mental gymnastics. You will learn to write in order to think, to encourage thought, to tease thought out of chaos or out of fright. You will write constantly, and continuously, at every stage, to name your topic and to find your way into it. You will learn to write past certainty, past prejudice, through contradiction, and into complexity. You will come to write out of your own self, and, eventually, even though you may be afraid of what your reader will say, you will learn to write in a way that will allow you to be heard. If you're to do all of this, you need to write every day, even if it's only for fifteen minutes a day.

If you commit yourself to writing at every stage, the process will look something like this: Early on, even before you've chosen a topic, you might make daily, dated journal entries, all of them in a thesis book (which might be separate pages on a pad that then go into a folder, or a bound notebook, or a computer file) about your thoughts, worries, interest in various topics. For example,

> *12/16/95: Today I'm thinking about how intrigued I've always been by the question of the use of model systems in studying biological development. I've always been aware that there are real disadvantages that come along with the advantages of this method—I wonder if I could do something with this for my dissertation. . . .*

When you first choose a topic, you'll spell out your preliminary hunches, ideas, questions:

> *1/15/96: What difference might it make if we were to use not rats, but elephants, as the model? What are the qualities of model system animals that have made us choose them so readily for much of our developmental research?*

As you start to accumulate data you'll not only take notes, but also begin to work with the data—talk back to it in writing, ask it questions, let the material suggest questions to you, and then you'll try to summarize your current understanding of it:

> *2/18/96: Organisms that share the desirable characteristic of having rapid embryonic development may share embryonic adaptations and constraints related to this trait—what difference does this make?*

As you go through, you'll take some trial runs at writing some bits of the dissertation:

> *4/2/96: The model systems approach, clearly an extraordinarily powerful way to analyze animal development, is based on certain assumptions. One is that we can extrapolate what we learn from a few model species to many other organisms. . . .*

You'll keep track of the flashes of insight you have that are spurred by your reading, as well as any serious misgivings you have:

2/3/96: What am I really trying to say here, and does it make sense?

At first you'll write in short stretches, and a bit farther on you may produce up to five pages a day (I'll teach you how to do this in chapter 3).

Developing Your Own Work Process

Each of you reading this book is unique, and no single prescription is going to be useful for all of you. I want to help you figure out how to devise the strategies that best suit who you are and how you work. The only rules there are in the dissertation-writing process are the useful ones you make up for yourself. You own this dissertation, and you are the one responsible for getting it from conception to birth; you can get there by whatever process works for you.

You begin by learning to pay attention to yourself as a writer, by writing at every possible stage of your work process. You'll note each day how your work has gone: how it felt, what you did and didn't accomplish; you'll ask yourself, in an internal dialogue that you record, what you think might have gotten in your way, what nagging question you've been trying to ignore, what you need to work on next, how you might have to change your work space, whether you like or hate your topic on this particular day. *You will take your own work habits as seriously as you take the material you're working on,* and you will scrutinize them frequently to see if they need revamping. If you get stuck (you discover you don't like composing on the computer, but you don't know what to do instead; or you are having trouble making time to work; or your writing is coming very, very slowly—too slowly to make your deadline), you'll seek consultation, first with yourself, in writing:

> *1/14/96 What is going on with my work? I'm having a terrible time clearing out my schedule. I'm doing favors for all my friends, and if I don't stop giving myself these excuses for not working, I'm never going to finish my dissertation! How can I make sure that I write before I talk on the phone, before I meet Harry for tea, before I comb the dogs?*

After that, you'll consult with your advisor, or with a friend who has lived through the process successfully, or perhaps with a counselor whom your university provides for such times. But first you'll confront the stuck place you're in by writing about it, researching it, asking yourself when it began (was it after you had a disappointing meeting with your advisor, or after you drank too much, or after you heard about that article that you're terrified will scoop your idea but haven't gotten up the courage to read yet?). You'll try varying your routine to see if another time, another place, another mode of writing works better. You'll think about whether it's time to make yourself a detailed outline or to play with another chapter for a while and give this one some time to rest. You may decide to consider the worrisome thought that you're barking up the wrong tree with a particular idea. All of these issues are food not only for thought, but for writing. And writing about them, as well as about whatever static you are experiencing in your head, will serve to resolve most of the issues that are bothering you. Writing will also be an essential tool in choosing the topic of your dissertation.

Choosing a Topic

What do you want from a thesis topic? Writing a dissertation is very much like being in a long-term relationship: there are likely to be some very good times and some perfectly dreadful ones, and it's a big help if you like what you've chosen. This particular relationship asks you to give up a lot of the other pieces of your life, to work like a dog, and to postpone gratification. There are people out there who seem to be able to make such sacrifices for a subject they're not particularly thrilled by, people for whom dissertation writing is the means to an end, to getting a degree. I admire your grit, if you're among them. If you choose your topic wholeheartedly, the writing process can be a wonderful opportunity for pleasure; if you don't, it's still possible to produce a good piece of work, and you may even surprise yourself and enjoy parts of the process.

Some people seem always to have known what they want to write their dissertations about. They are the lucky ones. They still need to find an advisor who will support their enterprise, but this is perhaps the easier task. Some, like me, have written their way through the same topic in various guises often enough so they know it's theirs for life. Some of you may have topics handed to you.

Some of the most fortunate thesis writers are driven to investigate and try to answer a question that is both professionally and personally compelling. To begin, stay with, and bring to completion a project this large, it's ideal to choose a topic that's really going to matter to you, enough to keep it going even on the dark days that are an inevitable part of the thesis process. How do you do this choosing? You follow your curiosity, and, if you're lucky, your passion. One person's passion may look strange to others, but for now you only have to please yourself. I've known writers who were entranced by the relative proportions of seeds in an archaeological dig, because they could read from those data how agriculture was carried out thousands of years ago. I was once so captivated by the possible sources for Chaucer's "Wife of Bath's Prologue" that I read in medieval Latin some of the most misogynistic literature in existence. These two projects would not necessarily turn on other people, but that doesn't matter.

You want to try to find what it is that you get excited thinking about, the academic subject for which you have substantial curiosity. As I've noted above, you can do this through writing. There may also be important clues in your academic career. Here's an example: As an undergraduate I was fascinated by questions of voice and authority; the subject of my senior thesis was the Fool in *King Lear*. As a graduate student in English I became interested in the sources of authority in Chaucer's work. The more general theme of authority gradually joined again in my work with the subject of voice—questions about who's the speaker, who gets to speak, what does it mean to have a voice, how does one grow one? Over the next fifteen years, my obsession with these issues led to a finished essay called "A Room of One's Own Is Not Enough," to work on memory, and to a dissertation on teaching writing in such a way as to promote the development of voice. All of this is visible, of course, only in retrospect: If you'd asked me twenty, or fifteen years ago, why I was writing on any of these topics, I wouldn't have known how to answer.

I'm not recommending that you necessarily try to understand your own pattern before you choose your thesis topic, or even that you necessarily have one; I'm suggesting you consider that such a pattern may exist, and allow yourself to go on a fishing expedition. This is how you will find out where your interest lies, where your curiosity leads you.

How do you do this? You think and write about the work you've done over the course of your academic career, and you remember which particular projects best held your interest, or excited you, or allowed you to have fun. See if these projects have anything in common. Even if you don't find such a pattern, you may still unearth some useful data. You may find out, for example, that your best papers were surveys—say, of all the novels by a particular author, rather than an analysis of a single work; or that you did your best thinking in papers that were comparative studies; or that you were strongest in heavily theoretical work; or that the lab projects that required the greatest attention to detail were the ones in which you had the greatest success.

Look not only at the subjects, but at the type of project— defined in a variety of ways—that you've succeeded at and enjoyed. My own dissertation, for example, is complicated organizationally, weaving together theoretical material from three different fields, but it is anchored by quite concrete case studies; my mind works best when I can continuously tie my theories to data. I've consulted with some people whose dissertations ranged from thoroughly grounded, in-depth studies of a single question and with others whose work involved multifaceted, theoretical explorations that cut across fields. You need to figure out which sort of undertaking best suits how you like to work.

Another good way to narrow your choice is to ask yourself what kind of writing and research by other people you find most interesting and enjoyable to read. You may like highly detailed work or more general treatments, or inductive versus deductive presentations; you may prefer many examples, or none, when you read theory; or you may opt for short chapters or long ones, a terse writing style or a more expansive one. All of these preferences are useful clues to the sort of dissertation you want to produce. And works by other people are also potentially useful models.

My thesis advisor knew how helpful a good model could be. One of her most useful suggestions was to point me toward a dissertation in an area related to mine that was a model of a doable thesis. This dissertation was mercifully short; it was also fascinating and well written. I knew that it was shorter and denser than my own would be, but throughout my own writing two essential things about that work stayed with me: I'd read an accepted thesis that was only 144 pages long, and it felt possible for me to produce that number of pages; and, quite as important, I could enjoy reading that dissertation. Ask your advisor to suggest some models; you'll probably learn something from them, and you'll also discover that some people not so different from you have managed to write dissertations.

Your advisor can also help you choose your topic by acting as a sounding board, limiting your grandiosity ("Do you really want to take on *all* of Henry James's novels in your thesis?"), helping you to clarify your main question, and talking with you about the politics of choosing a topic. Why do I use a word like "politics" here? Because your choice of topic can be central in determining your professional future, beginning with whether or not you'll get a job in the current market. I'm not suggesting that you choose your topic solely, or even primarily, on this basis. If you do, at the worst you could wind up feeling like you've prostituted yourself, and you may not produce a good piece of work. But you also risk ending up with neither a piece of work you can be proud of nor a job.

When I was in graduate school I knew a young man who was enchanted by the work of Robert Louis Stevenson. When he decided to write his thesis on Stevenson, the rest of us sat around shaking our heads, sure that such a nonacademic topic would doom him for the rest of his career. Yet he's the one among our group who occupies a named chair in the English Department at Harvard, while serving as a housemaster, so he can hardly be said to have been punished for daring to go with his passion, rather than with one of the more politically correct topics of the times. In the bull market of the 1960s, Robert Kiely could choose to write on Stevenson and still get a fine academic position; it's not at all clear that anyone could do so today. You may have to investigate where the jobs are in your field: if there are six positions in the country each year for Shakespeare scholars, you may want to write a thesis that broadens your possibilities; if you're lucky, perhaps you can figure out how to write part of it on Shakespeare, or you can promise yourself that your first article after you've finished will be about your new interpretation of *Macbeth*. Bribes like this are useful: "When my thesis is done I'll write the book [play, poetry, music . . .] that I really want to write." You'll have to remind yourself of your future reward often if you choose a topic that may not be your first choice but that is a nice, practical topic.

There's another, more playful way of choosing your topic, once you've bumbled around for a while and have some idea of your direction. Here's what you do: Imagine yourself deciding to go with the topic you've been considering. Now imagine finishing your dissertation and holding it in your hand. Ask yourself, "What shall I name this creation?" Try naming it; play with titles that are clearly too outrageous, and see which ones delight you. At the very least you'll have fun with your work; at the most you might be able to clarify and focus for yourself what you really want to write about. You might even want to give this exercise a try right now, and dream up the most outlandish titles you can. And, of course, write them down.

If you are a science dissertation writer, you're more likely to be given a topic, perhaps a piece of your advisor's larger research project. Or you will have to find some area in your field of interest that hasn't yet been researched, or, in a field like engineering or math, to invent or discover a technique or a theorem that's new or that has not been proved. You have to deal with the terror that you might work for years on a problem and never arrive at a solution. It may help to know that there have been successful science dissertations that explored why a given promising-looking avenue of inquiry failed; these studies do a public service by keeping others from wandering down the same dead-end paths. As a scientist you are playing a higher-stakes game than the English or history scholar, who knows (at least somewhere in her head) that if she works on a topic in earnest for long enough, she'll very likely be able to grind out a thesis. But you probably became a scientist in part for the excitement of the chase, and if and when you win, you win big: creating a successful lab experiment, inventing an original technique, discovering something surprising about embryological development, proving a new theorem. Once you get such a result, the moment of triumph is pretty clear, and the rest of the dissertation process is relatively easy. The sense of "I've got it!" can be much more subtle and elusive in dissertations in other fields.

Doing Research

How you do research varies widely from field to field: The biologist experiments in her lab, studying organisms with her eyes, electron microscopes, or biochemical assays. The anthropologist travels across the world to plunk himself down in the midst of another culture, to absorb it by thought, feeling, and senses, and then he transforms that experience into a new theory by thinking and getting a feeling about it. The historian searches old records, hoping to confirm her hunch of what an event was, to find the chink in the wall that separates her from the past, and if and when she finds it, she begins her own reconstruction. All of these activities are research; some of them use, or can make use of, writing. But sooner or later, all of these researchers will have to transform the results of their searches into written documents that explain those results. The discussion of specific research techniques is best undertaken with your advisor and your committee members, who are acquainted with the particular procedures of your field. Because of this, and because at least as many people get stuck writing up their results as doing research, I will focus here more on the psychology of research, and not on the details of how you will do it.

I probably won't ever forget the research I did for my first dissertation, the one I gave up on. This work, in medieval literature, consigned me to endless hours of sitting in the Bryn Mawr library stacks, looking out through leaded glass windows, dying of boredom, while I tried to return my attention to the work at hand—laboriously translating and reading the medieval Latin misogynistic texts of St. Jerome, which were among the sources of Chaucer's "Wife of Bath's Prologue." What I found genuinely interesting about this material was the very odd way in which Chaucer used his source; to make my point I needed to know the small details of the original text. What ultimately kept me from completing this thesis was the same failure of nerve that kept me mired in the details: the leap into speculation, into my own ideas about what Chaucer was doing, did not feel like "real research" to me; it was too much fun, too exciting, and too creative. To me "research" meant "serious," "tedious," "painful," and both the dry pedantry of the Bryn Mawr English Department in the 1960s and my own neuroses supported this misapprehension. Finally, the pain got to be too much for me. What I didn't know then—what I learned later by working on the thesis I did finish—was that ongoing writing could have helped me with both the details and the creative thinking that go into true research. I thought at the time *that if it wasn't tedious, it wasn't real research;* if the library work was mingled with my own creative juices, it wasn't real research. "Real research" was supposed to mean pain. I'd like to spare you this unnecessary misconception as you research your thesis.

If, instead, you think of research as active inquiry into a subject in order to work on it using the singular quality of your own intelligence, some things begin to be clear: "research" is not merely a matter of accumulating data that you then swallow; that is a relatively passive occupation. Research requires that your mind engage with the material, ask it questions, and act upon it in such a way as to change the material—and, incidentally, yourself. Otherwise the thousands of theses on Shakespeare would make no sense at all; it would make no sense that one of the best essays I've ever read on *King Lear* was written by a Harvard freshman. Research turns out to be not what I imagined it to be as I sat, suffering, in the Bryn Mawr library stacks, not a process of passive accumulation, but a thoroughly active one.

On Ownership

What does "ownership" of your writing mean? It means that your writing belongs, for better or for worse, to you, and you alone. If you screw up your courage to write, it is essential that your ownership of that writing be respected by your audience— of one or a thousand. Not necessarily agreed with, but respected. Your committee members can decide whether your body of writing constitutes an acceptable dissertation; a publisher or journal editor will decide whether it will reach a wider audience; any reader can like your writing or not, agree with it or not, understand it or not. But it is still yours. You get to decide what you're going to say, how you're going to say it, whom you're going to allow to read it. Other people own their responses to it, but you own the writing.

Your ownership of your dissertation means that you are stuck with it for life. In some ways, your doctoral dissertation is the most important (even if not the most famous, or the best) piece of work you'll do; in the course of producing it you learn how to be a scholar, and you may come to believe that you are one. If your topic is the best sort, it will also be seminal: you'll develop aspects of it in your future work for many years to come. And, at least initially, your topic will define your professional identity on the job market. You'll be surprised by the number of times you'll refer in various contexts to "what I wrote my dissertation about." It's therefore better if you write about something that's of deep and abiding interest to you, in a way that meets your own standards of intellectual integrity. But you may be surprised by how much you are able to invest deeply even in an assigned or instrumental topic.

About Maxims

The last thing I want to address in this chapter is the usefulness of superstition. Several of my writing clients have talked about how helpful they've found my "aphorisms" at times of struggle with their writing, and I find myself squirming at this feedback, because it makes me feel as if I'm dispensing small cans of advice to drink. What I hope is useful about these aphorisms—for example, Ruth Whitman's "Write first"—is their potential as personal maxims. We all need prompts that we devise to carry us through the hard times, to remind us that we've been here before and have gotten through it, to remind us that we can come to know what strategies work best for us.

I've sprinkled maxims liberally throughout my writing life, from the prompt that comes up on the screen when I turn on my computer, "Remember credibility," to the poems that hang framed next to my desk. Elizabeth Bishop's "One Art" reminds me that life is finite, so I'd better get on with the current project; another, quite silly poem tells me that writing is also about play. And on days when I'm tempted to fill up my writing time with the endless chores of life, I say Ruth's phrase, "Write first," over and over to myself.

What you need to figure out for yourself are the words that you most need to hear, words that you have to remember in order to get your writing done. They can be as awful as "My dog will love this thesis," as silly as "What do you call the lowest-ranked Ph.D. recipient at graduation?" "Doctor." You might remind yourself that "Living (and writing) well is the best revenge." Maxims can be reminders and offer encouragement. If you think and write about them, you'll discover the maxims that are your own.

2

Choosing an Advisor
and a Committee

Your Advisor

CHOOSING AN ADVISOR is one of the most important decisions you make in the dissertation process: it's up there with choosing a topic. In an ideal world your advisor would be a mentor, an expert in your field, a coach, an editor, and a career counselor; someone to guide, teach, and encourage you from the first glimmer you have of "the Right Topic" to your happy acceptance of a job offer from the institution of your choice. There are, however, few human beings who can fill that entire job description. (That is why you need a dissertation committee—even though all of its members together won't do the job perfectly either.)

How do you choose your advisor and your committee members, and what sorts of things do you need to pay attention to? Especially in the early stages of your professional life, it's useful to have at least one person who can teach you the ropes of your profession. Such a guide can encourage you to move out into the professional world and show you how to navigate in it, criticize you kindly when you need it, and act as your advocate both within your own department and out in the larger academic world. She will introduce you to colleagues, help you figure out what journal to send your first paper to, keep you from despair when it's not accepted, and push you to revise and resubmit it. In a perfect universe you would have such a person as your dissertation advisor; failing this, one or more of the members of your thesis committee may take on the mentor role, but it's not absolutely necessary. Even without a good mentor, you can still write a fine dissertation, survive, and prosper professionally.

In the real world there are important political considerations in choosing an advisor. In the academy, genealogy matters: one lab I visited actually had a "family tree" hanging on its wall, a map of the lab director's dissertation director, his "siblings"—other people whose dissertations were directed by the same "parent"—and his "children," his own advisees. You may find this ludicrous, but such things matter in many academic circles. You can find sixty-year-old, long-tenured professors who are still referred to as "Professor X's students." So consider carefully how much you want and need, for the sake of your potential academic career, to find an advisor whose name will matter in the job market.

Students in the laboratory sciences have some other things to take into account. There may be a very close link between choosing your advisor and choosing your topic: you often go into a lab to work on some aspect of whatever that lab does or is funded to do, and you may not get to choose the piece you work on. If you are entering a lab, it's also essential to check out who your lab mates are, because they will be important parts of the environment in which you work. Your choice of advisor may also determine your access to specific equipment, techniques, and facilities. If Professor Q holds the keys to the DNA lab, and you want to study DNA, how brilliant or kind he is may be of less concern than his connections.

You need to consider several other factors in choosing an advisor in any field. Check out the person's reputation among students. Such information is readily available on the graduate student grapevine. Another way to find out—indirectly but effectively—is to count how many successful "offspring" your potential advisor has; that is, what percentage of her students finish their degrees. Does this person appear to favor women students? Men? Where do her students go after they finish a doctorate with her? Ask her current or former students what she expects from her advisees, what her standards are, and then think realistically about whether you can live up to them.

Famous advisors are a mixed blessing. The advantages are obvious. But remember that such academics often spend a lot of time away from their own institutions, giving lectures, serving on committees, and the like, and they may not be easily available to you when you need their help. My first dissertation advisor was quite famous, but I quickly discovered that her students often had a hard time graduating, and that she appeared to compete with them and put obstacles in their paths. I remember the moment at which I realized that if I remained her advisee, I'd never finish. If choosing a politically advantageous, famous advisor makes it unlikely that you'll complete your degree, it's clearly not worth it.

Does your advisor have to be an expert in the field of your dissertation? In the sciences the answer is almost always yes. I hear stories of professors in other fields who meet every other important criterion but say, "But, of course, I don't know the literature on Austen, . . . semiotics, . . . the Civil War." Does this matter? Yes, but there are circumstances in which it might still make sense to choose Professor J, who is not an expert in your field but is bright, conscientious, decent, and helpful to students (and has a fine reputation as a thesis coach), over Professor K, the world expert who is awful to students and does nothing to help them find employment. Your choice has certain ramifications for your own responsibilities in the thesis process, and it's best to be aware of them from the beginning.

If you decide to go with Professor J, you'll trade someone who has expertise in your field and could, if he wished, make it readily available to you, for a different, probably more essential quality. (Professor K may have expertise, but it's not at all clear he'd share it with you.) With Professor J you'll have to go off and find other sources of expertise, but you'll also have the deeply gratifying, if sometimes frustrating, experience of being alone on the trail. You take the risk of reinventing the wheel, because Professor J can't say to you, "Oh yes, that's a lovely idea, but M has already published a major book on it." You'll have to do that scouting around for yourself.

Check what your potential advisor's calendar looks like over the time you expect to be working on your thesis. If she's planning a sabbatical leave during that time, you might want to choose someone else.

Once you've ascertained that J's or K's students do, in fact, finish, and that most of them do well after graduation, and that J and K will be in town during your crucial thesis time, you need to make the most important decision: can you work well with either of them, or learn to? Personality styles matter, and much as you might want to work with J, who has a good track record, is well connected, and is kind, if you seem to get on each other's nerves every time you meet, you might decide to reconsider.

Your Committee

If you thought choosing an advisor was complicated, you'll be surprised by the complexity of composing your dissertation committee. Your advisor may be able to help with this; in particular, he ought to know the local rules about what constitutes a legal committee. (If he doesn't, consult people in your department, or in the graduate student office.) One way of covering all the bases is to have on your committee (which is often composed of three people) someone else who is thoroughly grounded in your field whom you don't want (or can't have) as your advisor. If possible, it's nice to avoid having people on the committee who are enemies. Dissertation committee meetings can be tense; you don't need the added burden of other people's bad vibes. And, more important, you don't want the long-standing feud between Professors X and Y to take the form of scrapping over your dissertation.

A good committee will provide you with an attentive audience for your ideas and your prose, and with the backing and support of several advisors who have your best professional interest at heart. A well-balanced committee might consist of, for example, someone whose strong point is theory, someone else who is very knowledgeable about the literature in your field, and a third person who is a careful and respectful editor. Aim for balance, and make sure that you get what you, as a writer and thinker, will find most useful and what you want most from your readers. Some dissertation writers like *very* attentive readers; others prefer to be left pretty much alone. Some like a person to try out ideas on; others prefer to work on ideas by themselves until they feel ready for public scrutiny. This is one of those times when it's not worth fantasizing about having a personality transplant.

One question that frequently comes up in choosing committee members is whether to pick someone from another institution. (You may know such a person from his writings, or by reputation, or by having met him at a conference.) Sometimes there are clear reasons to choose someone from the outside: only two people at your own university are appropriate to oversee your work, or a particular outsider can bring special things to the process, or maybe there is a political situation in your department that an outsider might help to defuse. There are also reasons against such a choice: an outsider, by his very position, will have little local political capital to spend on your behalf, and he may be harder to communicate with. On the other hand, if you've chosen someone who is well known in your field, she may be quite useful politically, and she might help to extend your network of professional contacts. Finally, if you're in a department that's dogmatic or one-sidedly ideological, and your own theoretical stance or subject is not welcome, it can be life-saving to have someone on your committee from the outside world, someone with a clearer view of the merits of your work.

Using Your Advisor Well

It's particularly important that you figure out how to talk with your advisor, how to be firm and reasonable at the same time, and how not to be railroaded into writing a dissertation that won't feel like your own. But at the same time you need to consider your advisor's point of view very carefully, to make sure that he isn't, perhaps, at least partly right in his comments or observations, and that you're not just being stubborn, conservative, or defensive. This is often a hard judgment to make.

Whether or not you're neurotic, if your advisor's idea of what you ought to write about feels truly impossible once you've scrutinized your own resistance or stubbornness, then don't do it. It probably won't work if you try. At the worst, you won't finish; even at the best, you'll get no pleasure from the work, and you risk not only a major waste of your time and energy, but also destroying your joy in, and enthusiasm for, your field of study and your own work. Remember that writing and finishing your dissertation is more important to you than to anyone else— and should be.

An advisor/advisee relationship is like other relationships. Most don't work perfectly at first, or all the time, but there must be enough goodwill on each side so that you can both try to make your relationship work (this doesn't mean that either of you can promise that you'll never be impossible). Your job is to get your advisor to help you as much and as effectively as possible. How do you do this?

• Establish clear guidelines and expectations on each side from the beginning ("I will get nervous if I hand you my writing and then don't hear from you for a month" or "You can phone me at home if you wish, but never after nine at night"). Don't expect your advisor to welcome your giving her your manuscript at the last minute; while you may like the excitement of eleventh-hour submissions, she may need to plan reading time.

• Be realistic about what your responsibilities in the thesis-writing process are, and don't expect your advisor to do your thinking or your work for you.

• Don't throw tantrums; that's unprofessional. Remember that you've engaged this person to help you improve your work, not to rubber-stamp it, and that you need him to tell you the truth as he sees it. You don't have to take his advice, but you do have to consider his suggestions with an open mind (this is hard to do, but it can be learned). You also need to behave like an adult even when you don't feel like one.

• But don't, under any circumstances, let yourself be abused. Speak up, politely but firmly: "When you write on my draft, 'This is garbage,' it makes it very hard for me to know where to begin, and I hear you saying that this will never be any good. I need you to do . . ."

• Stay in charge of your own writing; remember you're the owner.

• Establish regular meeting times, and stick to them. Decide between you which reasons are sufficient for changing, or cancelling, a session (for example, a sick child, but not any kind of social engagement, unless one of you has been invited to the White House or the Vatican); keep the reasons to a minimum. Meet even if you've written nothing—in fact, *particularly* if you've written nothing.

• Settle explicitly what your advisor is, and isn't, willing to read. Some want to see only coherent drafts, not sloppy zero drafts. Others will ask to see much earlier versions. Most will not want manuscripts that come as total surprises; that is, versions that the student considers final but has never bothered to show to the advisor. A careful advisor won't permit this last scenario.

On Dissertation Paranoia

Sometimes writing a dissertation is a bit like having a serious, but not mortal, illness: it takes enormous energy to sustain life, you have to take very good care of yourself so you don't collapse, and your defenses—in this case not white blood cells, but psychological defenses—are sky high. One symptom of this "illness" is "dissertation paranoia," the powerful, not totally rational feeling that other people are out to harm you, and that you must be vigilant and fierce in order to protect yourself and your work. Paranoia, of course, is not paranoia when someone really *is* out to get you. Clearly this can be a delicate judgment to make. One needs defenses to survive, but when they're overly vigilant, they may work against you: you may bridle at a good piece of advice from your advisor that would improve your dissertation, because you perceive her motives to be sadistic. Dissertation paranoia, fortunately (unlike the sort that one suffers if one has a serious mental illness), is time limited: it tends to disappear when your final draft has been accepted.

Troubles with Your Advisor

Because most intense relationships are complex and imperfect, you and your advisor may sometimes run into trouble. Here are some possible scenarios, and some possible solutions:

• *Your advisor doesn't listen to what you can and want to do in your dissertation; instead, she keeps insisting on her sense of what you should be working on.* Tackle this conflict from two different directions. First make sure that what you're feeling is proper ownership, and not dissertation paranoia. If you are pretty sure it's the former, make an earnest attempt to explain what you're attempting to do in your dissertation. If your advisor still won't buy it, you'll have to decide if you can, for political reasons, do what she wants, without either getting ulcers or stopping working. If not, you may have to consider switching advisors (which is a good reason for settling this kind of issue early on).

• *Your advisor competes with you.* This is a particularly difficult situation to be in at this stage of your career. It's not fair, it's not kind, but you may be stuck with it anyway. You'll know if this is what's happening if your advisor is always trying to put you down or one-up you, often comparing your ideas (disparagingly) to his. Once again, you have to appraise the situation carefully: First, are you pretty sure this is what's happening? Second, if you are, are there enough other advantages to this particular person so it's worth thickening your skin, using this experience as practice for the academic jungle? A third calculation, of course, is whether you think your well-connected, competitive advisor will consider you enough of a feather in his cap so that later on, he'll work to advance your professional interests.

• *Your advisor disparages you, and you end up feeling lousy about yourself and your work.* One of the hardest lessons to learn is that no one can "make you" feel bad about yourself: you have a choice about whether to take other people's disparagement to heart. Having said this, I also acknowledge that it is terribly demoralizing to have an advisor who runs you down. If you feel up to it (and this is a very delicate judgment call) you might decide to take your advisor on. But I think very few thesis writers can carry this off successfully, for a variety of reasons (the most important one being the imbalance of power in even the best of advisor/student relationships). If you decide to tough the relationship out (and most writers will, because it's hard to change advisors midstream), it's absolutely essential to develop a network of other people who will encourage and support you and your dissertation, as an antidote to your advisor's malevolence.

• *Your advisor is hard to get hold of, doesn't return your calls, and is often inaccessible or off on the other side of the continent or the world.* Try being very, very clear about when you think you'll need help; ask how you can best get in touch; and then, at the inaccessible times, if you must contact her, use every mode available—phone, E-mail, fax, FedEx—to try to reach her. (And keep a paper trail of your attempts, should you later be accused of failing to communicate.) Ideally, when you do your initial research about advisors, other students will tell you that Professor X tends to disappear at crucial moments, and you will, if it's possible within the limitations of your department, pick someone else (or at least be forewarned). Make sure that you stay in contact with other readers and advisors, formally or informally, so that you can get the help you need. You could also form a support group of Professor X's orphaned advisees.

• *Your advisor criticizes you so strongly that it takes you weeks to get back to work after a meeting.* You can't afford to take weeks off after each time you meet. Try writing about your meetings right afterward, or write your advisor a poison-pen letter that you don't send, or go work out in the gym—but find some way to release the powerful feelings that these meetings produce in you. Even better, use your anger to fuel your work; it can be even more effective than caffeine. You might also want to think about how you present yourself and your work. (I'm not trying to blame the victim, but I have known thesis writers who offered their work to others so apologetically that they inspired readers with any sadistic tendencies to go on the attack.) The hardest job is sorting out appropriate criticism from nastiness, so it helps to engage others, such as your fellow students/victims, in this effort. Get outside feedback from other professors, not necessarily within your own department or university, as a reality check. And remember that your best revenge is living, and writing, well.

• *Your advisor comes on to you.* This is grounds for a lawsuit. At the very least be careful about when and where you meet. Be firm and clear about this behavior not being acceptable. Document the person's actions if you possibly can; ask others if they've had the same experience (it's common for a person who carries on in this way to do so with more than one student); and, should you decide to press charges, choose your time carefully. This is one of the worst situations an advisee can come up against. See if you can switch advisors.

These are all, in increasing order of severity, bad and worst-case scenarios. In my profession I tend to hear more of them than most people do, so I realize that my experience is skewed. These awful situations are rare, and you are unlikely to run into them, but such things do happen in the human world of academia, and you may have to deal with them. Remember that, even in these out-of-control cases, even in a relationship of unequal power, you still retain some control over your work, your feelings, and your life.

• • •

Think hard about how you can best use other people's talents and input. Then choose an advisor and a committee to match your needs as closely as possible. Don't try to pick what you think you *ought* to need, but, on the basis of your own past experience, what you will actually find helpful. With good fortune and some advance planning, you will be able to avoid some of the worst-case scenarios, defuse others, and, even in the most extreme cases, continue to own your work and your integrity.

(One of my acquaintances who had the dissertation advisor from hell wrote a first-rate thesis in record time by repeating over and over to herself, "Don't get mad, get even!") Most advisors value the privilege of their position and do not abuse their power, and many students leave graduate school having forged a valuable lifelong professional relationship with their dissertation advisors.

3

Getting Started Writing

THIS CHAPTER aims to help you get started writing. When I worked at Harvard's Writing Center, we joked that the single most useful piece of equipment for a writer was a bucket of glue. First you spread some on your chair, and then you sit down.

Thoughts on the Writing Process

In the interests of your doing more than just sitting there, I want to think out loud for a bit about the writing process, and how it doesn't and does work. I am about to violate an important behavioral principle: "Never teach someone how to do something by showing them the wrong way to do it." Let's look at what they taught me in school about how to write. First you chose a topic, perhaps off a list, perhaps at your teacher's suggestion, perhaps out of the air or by looking at which shelf in the library still had books available on it. Then you researched the topic (this step seemed to involve a lot of index cards). Then you thought about your topic. (I've always imagined here a cartoon of someone sitting at a desk, with an empty word balloon attached to her head.) Having thought, you made an outline for your paper, then wrote, starting with I,1 on your outline, fleshing it out, making sure you had a good topic sentence for each paragraph. You proceeded through the outline in order, and when you finished, and capped the paper off with a final, summarizing paragraph, you let the paper rest for a day (sort of like bread dough), then came back, checked the grammar, spelling, transitions, and diction, and cleaned all of them up. Then you were done.

I don't think this model worked. Much of the time it led to neat, clean, boring papers, often to empty ones with good form. It very rarely produced papers that were deeply thoughtful, that had strong and distinctive voices and styles, that raised as many questions as they answered, that made you read, and reread, and then dream about the topic. I want to teach you to write using a method that does all these things.

If you look at a piece of finished writing, all neat and orderly, and know nothing about how it actually came about, you might deduce that it was created using what Arlo Guthrie calls "the good old-fashioned boring model." But this isn't how good, finished writing usually occurs, and even when it does, such a method may not have been the best or most satisfying way of producing it. In her essay "Elusive Mastery: The Drafts of Elizabeth Bishop's 'One Art,'" Brett Candlish Millier looks at the seventeen drafts of Bishop's poem in order to discover how exquisite writing *really* gets done. The most shocking thing I found out from reading Bishop's drafts is that her first draft looks nearly as awful as my own first-draft poems do; it's what Bishop does after that—and how many times she does it—that makes all the difference.

How does one really begin to write? William G. Perry Jr. has described the process succinctly: "First you make a mess, then you clean it up." If you think about the implications of this statement, you quickly realize that how you write is up for grabs: no more neat outlines with Roman numerals to follow, no elegant topic sentences for each paragraph, maybe not even any clear sense of where you're going. If you're not going to feel like you're in free fall, you're going to need some other strategies. What will get you through the beginning stages of this new model are a few behavioral principles, an understanding of good addictions, and a plan for producing messy writing every day.

When you sit down to begin a piece of writing, your first aim ought to be to make a mess—to say anything that comes to your mind, on the subject or off it, not to worry at all about whether your stuff is connected logically, to play with your subject the way you used to build mud pies, to do no fine detail work, to spell poorly if that's your natural inclination, and to generally forget about standards altogether (even about split infinitives!). I suspect many writing blocks come about because people aren't used to playing in the mud when they write; they think writing is a neat, clean endeavor. I don't.

You may think I'm asking you to be an irresponsible, uncaring writer. But I'm really asking you to try something that will have just the opposite effect, if you see it through. The writing process I have in mind has two parts to it, a first, "cooking," making-a-mess part; and a second, compulsive, clean-up-the-mess part. If you do only the first part, you will indeed end up with a messy, irresponsible product you won't want to acknowledge as your own. If you do both parts, though, I believe you'll be able to produce stronger, more imaginative writing that you'll feel proud to own.

When I suggest that you make a mess in writing, I don't

mean that you have to go out of your way to make your writing disorganized, or uncommunicative, just that you need to control your worry in the first part of the writing process; it helps to do this if you think of your aim as making mud pies or sandcastles, rather than stone buildings. You are making a sketch, not a finished oil painting.

What ought you stop worrying about? It would be nice if you could completely ignore your spelling (it only needs to be good enough so you can figure out what you wrote, should you decide to reread your writing). It would be even better if you could ignore sentence structure. Concentrate on what you're trying to say, and see how many different ways you can say it. You may find that your meaning, as well as your style, will be shifty at this point. You don't need to worry at all during this first stage about overall organization; I certainly hope you won't feel compelled to begin at the beginning and move from there to the middle and the end of your piece.

If the writing doesn't sound good to you while you're writing it, it's fine to make a note to yourself about this. (I find it useful to keep up a running dialogue with myself about the questions and problems I've having while I'm writing.) I often put that commentary right in the midst of my text, using square brackets, or a different color ink or pencil, so that when I come back to revise, I can recognize and engage quickly with the problems I've already noted. I don't stop to hunt for words when I'm in this messy phase; if I can't get just the right word, I list the three or four alternatives/choices/words/senses, just like this. I can stop and open the thesaurus while I'm working on a second draft, when doing that won't threaten to interrupt the flow of my thoughts and feelings.

The main goal for this first stage of writing is to keep it going, to keep the interesting and alive associations in your brain sparking. You don't want to do anything at this point that's going to get in their way. Writing from an outline sometimes short-circuits the imaginative part of writing altogether. Obsessing about technical details can slow it down or stop it altogether. If you need to think about your writing in terms of perfection, perhaps it will help you to know that making a mess is not only functional, but essential for creating that perfect final product you have in mind. In chapter 4 I'll talk about cleaning up the mess.

Using Behavioral Principles

There are only a few simple behavioral principles you need to know. First, you need to know the difference between negative and positive reinforcement. It's possible to train ourselves to do things by punishing ourselves each time we do something wrong, but this method is both inefficient and inhumane. Positive reinforcement, rewarding ourselves each step of the way as we accomplish a series of small goals on the way to achieving the large one (what animal trainers call "shaping"), is both more pleasant and much more effective. (If you've tried, God forbid, to train a puppy by beating it, you'll know that you can end up with a docile dog, but not one with any spirit or joy. Puppies who are trained with praise and treats grow into lively, obedient dogs.)

How do you translate these observations into a process that rewards writing? You set up goals for yourself that are doable, and then you reward yourself with the legal treat of your choice, whatever that is: a run with a friend; a cup of coffee at your favorite café; a half hour to read a novel, listen to music, or chat on the phone—you'll know what your own pleasures are. You try to steer clear of self-blame and critical lectures (from other people, too), and of bad-mouthing what you've written. And you won't put yourself in circumstances in which you repeatedly fail to write. (I have actually had the following conversation with a client: "Where do you do your writing?" "At the kitchen table." "How does it work?" "I never get anything done there.")

You also need to practice two kinds of rewards—the simple sort I've described above, and also a more sophisticated kind known as the Premack Principle, or "Grandma's mashed potatoes law": "No dessert until you've eaten your mashed potatoes." This principle says you can reinforce a desired behavior by pairing it with another behavior that you value highly and will do for its own sake. Translated into a strategy for writing, it means you will find some behavior you don't want to live without—say you don't feel like a day is complete unless you've read the newspaper—and then not allow yourself to do it until you've accomplished your writing goal for that day. One of the oddest and most exciting possibilities of this sort of reinforcement is that once you've established a good writing habit, the writing itself may become the reward, the reinforcement.

The other strategy I want to emphasize is this: make very, very sure that you set realizable goals for yourself; that is, avoid assigning yourself a piece of work that is too large to accomplish. It is much better to say that you'll write two sloppy pages a day and actually do them than to set your goal at ten pages and not write anything because the task is too overwhelming even to begin. If you set yourself up to fail, you will soon discover that you're writing less. And less. And still less.

It's also a mistake to push yourself to do more than your daily goal. If you try to do this, you'll often find yourself unable to meet your goal the next day.

Write even if you feel sluggish, even if you feel lousy, even if you feel like you have nothing to say. You can still begin to get a process started, and to learn about your writing rhythm. Days when you're productive and the writing feels like it writes itself will most likely alternate with others, when it feels like you've never written anything worthwhile and never will. When I give talks about writing, the line that consistently draws the most laughter of recognition is "Most people would rather wash the bathroom floor than write." The best way to get into a good writing rhythm is to *write every day,* except maybe your birthday, or the queen's. You can define "every day" as you please—seven days a week, or only weekdays, or at least five days out of every seven—so long as you define what you intend to do in advance and don't keep changing the rules as you go along. Don't decide, for instance, not to write on a morning when you don't feel like writing. In this respect, too, writing is very much like running: if you wait to decide whether or not to run until you wake up in the morning, the odds are you won't get your shoes on and your body out the door. The only way to run or to write regularly is to make a rule for yourself that you allow yourself to break only rarely.

About Creating a Writing Addiction

Addictions get pretty bad press. But we often overlook the human propensity for addictions: book collectors have them, opera buffs have them, those who garden beautifully, or cook well, or do anything with passion have them. There are bad addictions and good ones. It's fine to be addicted to exercise, to being out in the air, to getting in touch with the world by reading the newspaper or listening to the news on the radio every day, to swimming, to gardening. Writing can be this kind of an addiction for some fortunate people, and, as with the others, the reason it can become an addiction is because it satisfies an essential need and gives pleasure. (Yes, I really *did* say *pleasure*.) What's the need?

For some of us, writing gives us a place to be with ourselves in which we can listen to what's on our minds, collect our thoughts and feelings, settle and center ourselves. For others of us it gives us a chance to express what would otherwise be overwhelming feelings, to find a safe and bounded place to put them. For some, it's like exercise: this is the way we warm up a muscle that we're going to be called upon to use. And the pleasure? For anyone who's ever had a running habit, it's easy to describe. The satisfaction of writing every day is very much like the satisfaction of a daily three-mile run. One begins, lives through a warmup, hits stride, has the experience of "being run" rather than "running," of a fluidity of motion that one no longer has to direct, and then, cooled down, can feel, "Now the rest of the day's my own. I've done what I most needed to do." And for those who've never run? Writing offers the pleasure of a deep, ongoing engagement in an activity that is meaningful, one where you know more at its end than you knew at its beginning.

Why do we get addicted? Because when something gives us intense pleasure, that pleasure works as a reinforcer; that is, it brings us back to the activity with greater and greater frequency. Positive addictions can also focus us; they have their own built-in motivation, complete with withdrawal symptoms. A few weeks into our work, one of my writing clients came in looking distressed; she said that she "felt antsy" and was wondering if it was because she hadn't had the time to write for the past few days. We poked around a bit looking for the possible cause of her distress, and we decided the absence of writing was probably it. The good news, of course, was that she'd managed to develop a self-perpetuating writing addiction very quickly.

So you need to begin to experiment with cultivating a writing addiction, with establishing patterns and changing them if they don't work. Even if you're terribly neurotic, and even if you never do become a true "writing addict," behavioral methods can still help you write. It is not necessary to feel joyous about writing in order to produce a good dissertation, or even to enjoy part of its creation. Try writing while you're working on your neuroses—and should you choose not to work on them, you will probably still feel a bit better if you get some work done.

Freewriting and Making a Mess

Here is how you can use freewriting to establish your writing addiction. You start with a very small task, learning to write for ten minutes every day, come hell or high water. I get a lot of raised eyebrows from new writing clients when I suggest this, and comments like "Ten minutes? At that rate it will take me ten years to finish my thesis!" I generally point out that so far they've been unable to write anything at all, and that ten minutes a day is a great improvement over that (mathematically it's an infinite improvement). It's certainly true that you can't write a thesis if you continue to write for *only* ten minutes a day, but this is a good way to begin. Despite this book's title, I recommend starting out by writing ten minutes a day because I think it works most quickly and easily to get you on track. Once you're doing that, you can work up to fifteen minutes and, gradually, to much longer stretches of writing. Anyone can write for ten minutes a day, particularly if one is freewriting; it's a task that's pretty well guaranteed to be doable. It's essential to begin your practice with a task you're sure to succeed at. There is nothing quite as effective at killing a dissertation as vowing to write eight hours every day and failing to—as anyone must—day after day. Ten minutes a day is a very effective way to establish a writing addiction.

How do you actually do your ten minutes a day of writing? By following the directions for freewriting laid down by Peter Elbow in *Writing Without Teachers*:

> Don't stop for anything. Go quickly without rushing. Never stop to look back, to cross something out, to wonder how to spell something, to wonder what word or thought to use, or to think about what you are doing. If you can't think of a word or a spelling, just use a squiggle or else write, 'I can't think of it.' . . . The easiest thing is just to put down whatever is in your mind. If you get stuck it's fine to write 'I can't think what to say, I can't think what to say' as many times as you want; . . . The only requirement is that you *never* stop.

Note the bass note: keep writing, no matter what; even if you hate it you can do it for ten minutes. And then see how much writing you've produced. Most people write, on average, about one or one and a half handwritten pages in ten minutes. What's very surprising is that even in such a short block of seemingly mindless writing (and here we come back to the power of the unconscious) you will occasionally, on rereading your words, find something interesting, something you didn't know before, or, maybe more accurately, something you didn't know you knew. Freewriting is one of those activities in which two and two sometimes add up to five. Obviously, even ten minutes of wonderful freewriting every day won't quite get you to where you want to go, so you need to learn how to increase your writing production. But you only need to think about taking further steps once freewriting has become a familiar, comfortable, and self-reinforcing process for you.

Using the freewriting, messy model works much better than conventional methods in two different ways: it causes you less pain while you're doing it, and it produces better writing. Here's what it looks like: Say you need to write something like a rough proposal for your thesis, and you're feeling pretty uncertain about both your choice of topic and how you're going to develop it once you know what it is. You sit down at your desk and begin to freewrite, putting down on the paper any thoughts, ideas, or feelings you may have around or about your general topic. You keep asking yourself questions in writing, such as "Do I want to pick this topic, which I know I can move through methodically to the end, and risk boredom and an ordinary thesis, or do I want to risk my professional neck by picking the maverick topic that excites me?" (There is no obvious answer to this question, by the way.) Other questions may occur to you, both around and inside your project: "Can I really do this thesis stuff, sustain interest long enough to write what amounts to a book?" "Will anyone want to read this when I'm done?" "How do I begin setting limits on a thesis about Anthony Trollope when he wrote so many books? What do I include? What do I leave out?" Or "What do I think the interesting questions are about Trollope's portrayal of his female characters?"

You do freewriting—inclusive, messy, not necessarily seeming to progress—every day, coming back to your own thoughts and feelings, seeing what the depths present you with each day. As you work on these iterations you will discover that your thoughts and feelings are becoming clearer, and your topic is becoming clearer. I don't think I've ever worked with a student who stuck with freewriting for whom this didn't happen.

Now it is time to work toward slightly more focused, less free writing that nevertheless moves along quickly, taps into the underground streams of your thought, and moves by rapid association to open up new ideas and new directions. The aim of not-quite-so-free writing is to use a bit more of your rational mind. You do this by setting yourself a somewhat more focused task at the outset, not "write about anything for ten minutes," but "write as fast as I can for the next ten minutes about one novel by Trollope, trying to focus on its politics," or "What's my best current guess about what shape this chapter is going to take?" or "What bothers me most about this chapter, and can I think of any answers to my worry?" In other words, you set yourself a sloppy topic, ask yourself a question to get you thinking along certain lines, and try to focus your scope from the whole world down to the issues of your thesis. Some of these questions that you paste, metaphorically, at the top of your page of writing will come out of the freewriting you've already done. But you will still sometimes want to follow your mind wherever it leads you, still use association, and still not worry if your thinking is divergent. Divergent thinking is what will ultimately produce some of the most interesting ideas in your dissertation.

Some writers might do better, in fact, to start with this slightly-less-free writing. Sometimes it's easier to write about "something" than about "anything." If you find yourself struggling unsuccessfully to turn out freewriting, try instead to do the somewhat more focused writing that I've described in the previous paragraph.

By now you ought to be able to write pretty quickly, and to focus your writing without strangling the flow. You've learned, on good days, how to use freewriting to improve the speed and the fluency of your writing, and to establish the channel between your thoughts and your writing, in order, as B. F. Skinner has put it, "to discover what you have to say." (I particularly like the gentle pun in his phrase: you will discover both what you have in you to say and also what you most need to say.) Where do you go from here, and how do you begin to accumulate writing at a rate that will permit you to finish your dissertation before your hundredth birthday?

Setting Your Daily Writing Goal

What you need to decide next is how you're going to set your daily writing goal. There are three ways to do this, and all three work, although not equally well. The first—let's call it the "sit there method"—is to say that you will write for a fixed amount of time, say two hours, every day. There are not a lot of people who can just write—not stare off into space, not get up to make five pots of coffee, not talk on the phone, but write continuously—for more than about two hours a day. You can write for a very long time on any given day, but the trouble is, you can't then do it again the next, and again, and again—and writing daily is the pattern that's best suited to finishing a dissertation. The second method, the inspiration method, is to plan on writing each day until you come up with one or two decent ideas. The third, the "many pages method," is to pick a reasonable number of pages and write that same number every day.

On the basis of my experience with lots of writers, I think the many pages method works best. If you fix an amount of time, as in the sit there method, it's possible to spend all or most of that time staring at the wall, and then you've both wasted time and produced nothing. The problem with the inspiration method is that no one has ideas every day; some writing days are deserts, yet it's important to write anyway. The advantage to the many pages method is that it rewards fast writing: writing about five pages can take between one and five hours. (I'm not talking about five polished pages, but rather five junk pages, very close to freewriting.) But with a goal of five pages, the faster you can do them, the sooner your time is your own; this method rewards learning to write faster, and from what I've seen, fast writing produces no worse results than slow writing does. This method also produces a large volume of writing, and at least *some* of it is likely to be useful. Play around with these various methods, and see which one suits your style best.

Let me describe the many pages method in a bit more detail, because I think most people will choose it. First, establish your natural daily number of pages by choosing a number arbitrarily, probably somewhere between three and six pages, and then trying to write that number of pages each day for a week. (Once again, if you're a runner, you know the feeling of the "natural number" from the way you decide how many miles to run each day.) When you've hit your natural number of pages, you will experience this sequence: some slowness getting in, for, say, the first page, then the sense that you've hit your stride and can just write along for a while, thinking things, following some byways, exploring, maybe even discovering a new idea or two. Then you'll come to a point at which you start to tire and feel like there's not much left in your writing reservoir for the day. This is the time to begin to summarize for yourself where you've been, to write down your puzzlements or unanswered questions, to do what Kenneth Skier, who taught writing at M.I.T. many years ago, calls "parking on the downhill slope": sketching out in writing what your next step is likely to be, what ideas you want to develop, or follow, or explore when you pick up the writing again the next day. This step will help you get started more easily each day, and it will save you an enormous amount of energy and angst.

If you write between three and six pages daily (you are allowed one day a week off—even God got one day off), you will find that you rapidly accumulate a lot of writing. Much of it will be what I call "junk writing"—it will not appear anywhere in your dissertation—but it is, nevertheless, important to have written it. Ideas don't emerge from most people's minds neatly, they rise up out of a quite chaotic soup, and you need to provide the proper medium for them to emerge from. As you go along, you'll move to less free writing and find your ideas developing and your arguments beginning to shape themselves. These pages will make up the first substantial piece of your dissertation, the zero draft. Your job is to keep writing, *every day,* keep accumulating those pages and gradually focusing them, dating them, keeping them in a notebook, or a computer file, or a literal file where you can easily lay your hands on them.

But here are my last two essential pieces of advice, as you sit down and get started writing.

The first: Don't waste words. Whenever you have an idea, a strategy, even a glimmer of an idea, *write it down*. Don't figure you'll remember it. Don't talk about it with someone before you've written it down. Have a place to put it—a notebook, a pocket computer, an index card you carry with you (finally, a use for those index cards you bought when you used the old-fashioned research and writing method); develop the habit of always writing down those bright ideas that come to you while you're on the run.

The second: I have been a very stubborn (my detractors call it "resistant") student all my life. But the bit of stubbornness I most regret was that for five years I failed to take my best writing teacher's advice. Ruth Whitman's words to me were very simple: "Write first." By this she meant, make writing the highest priority in your life. But she also meant those words literally; that is, write before you do anything else in your day. I saw how she translated this maxim into action when we were staying in the same house during a poetry workshop she led. There were eleven miles of beach right out the door of that house that sat on an island off the coast of South Carolina, but Ruth didn't begin her day with a lovely walk on the beach. Nor, for that matter, with any casual conversation with the rest of us. She woke up, made herself some coffee, and retreated to her bedroom, where she spent the next two hours reading and writing. Then she emerged, ready to teach us what she knew about writing poetry. Being quite literal-minded, I had to see her in action if I was to believe and understand what Ruth Whitman meant when she said, "Write first!" I came home from that workshop, rearranged my clinical schedule in order to start writing first thing four days a week; the other three days I manage to tuck it in some other time of the day. I'm sustained by the feeling that I have finally managed to put my own writing first, and I hope you will hear this particular piece of fine advice faster than I did.

4

From Zero to First Draft

BY NOW YOU'VE WRITTEN a lot of pages, and most of them are a mess. How do you begin to turn what you have written into a true first draft? This is one of the most anxiety-producing stages in the thesis-writing process, second only to beginning. You've been writing for quite a while, but it may not be clear that you have anything to say or to show for your effort—just a pile of messy, at times incoherent, writing. This chapter is about how to turn that chaos and mess into a piece of writing that has a shape (although not necessarily a final one) and some semblance of an argument. This is the stage at which you can begin to answer the questions, "What is this material about? What question am I asking? How might I answer it?"

The Zero Draft

You can think about where you are in your dissertation by considering the definitions of "zero" and "first draft." I first heard about zero drafts from Lois Bouchard, a talented writer and teacher of writing. What she meant by "zero draft" was this:

This is a rich soup, and that's all. You don't have to judge it, query it, make much of a fuss about it. It just is, and you can let it be. And you don't have to show it to anyone. Or this is a starting point, and not defined. Nothing you've written here is carved in stone. Nothing is even necessarily usable, but you've got something. It's called a zero draft.

A "zero draft" may or may not really exist, depending on how you write. It can be the name you give your accumulated pages the first time they begin to have any shape at all, although they are still so messy that it would be presumptuous to call them "a first draft," yet are clearly more organized than pure chaos.

The zero draft is the point where it becomes possible to imagine, or discern, a shape to your material, to see the method in your madness. This draft can take many forms: it can be a very tentative, prose outline, or a declaration of direction: "O.K., I'm beginning to see what this is all about. My question is rising up out of this mess, and I seem to keep coming back to it in many ways. . . . Here are the questions I'm following, and here are some tentative beginnings to answers to these questions (some of them mutually contradictory)."

Or "I've written about three different kinds of fictional worlds over and over during the last month, but now I see that there are really only *two* kinds, that a and b are really part of one kind, that can be described as . . . What I'm going to do now is to set up a chapter structure that compares the two sorts, and read back through this mess, culling useful examples and ideas."

Or "A month ago I drew up an outline for this chapter, and since then I've allowed myself to wander all over the place. Now I think the outline wasn't quite right, and I need to change it in the following ways: . . . Here's the sort of shape I want it to have—and now on to the first draft."

The First Draft

A first draft is your attempt to produce a complete, albeit very imperfect, version of what you're ultimately going to say. And, unlike the zero draft, it will be subject to your analytical and critical scrutiny. You will ask questions that are out of bounds for the zero draft, such as "Is this right? Do I have any evidence for this statement? Does this argument work?" And you will build from it.

A first draft has both more form and a different feel than your zero draft. You'll know that you've reached it when you see that what you've been writing has real content—and perhaps a rudimentary shape—that it has gone from being a mess to being a document. Having a first draft means you don't have to start from scratch each time you write; you may have several paths, but you're no longer in uncharted territory. Your first draft is a piece of writing from which you can extract some sort of coherent outline. It begins to answer a question, or questions, and proves that you have made some progress toward defining it, or them. It may have the wrong shape, but it has a shape you can work on.

Getting to Your First Draft

If you have an accumulation of freewriting or a zero draft, turning out a first draft is a matter of finding ways of building on or fleshing out ideas you have already put down in writing.

Here are some strategies for getting started:

- Pick out words, phrases, or sentences in the writing you've got that seem interesting, or provocative, or resonant, and try writing beginning with them.
- Ask yourself,
  "What stands out for me most in what I've written?"
  "Is there an argument in this mess?"
  "What point do I want to make?"
  "Is what I've said here true?"
  "Do I still believe this?"
- Try writing, repeatedly, in five- or ten-minute spurts of freewriting, an answer to the question "What am I *really* trying to say in this argument/chapter/section?"

Asking Questions

How to get from zero to first draft is intimately connected to how you hone your question. The answer to "What's my question in this dissertation?" doesn't get settled for good in your thesis proposal, in your outline, or the first time you begin writing. The most unnerving and exciting part of this next stage of your writing is honing your question or questions.

We ask ourselves questions all the time: "What's going on here?" "Why am I so confused?" "What did he mean by that?" "How am I going to get from here to there?" You need to take this ability and apply it to working on your dissertation as you learn to carry on an ongoing dialogue with writing, with your reader, and with yourself.

The abilities to ask questions and to learn that the question you ask is at least as important as the answer you get may be the most important skills you can get from a good education. What may be new for you when you write a thesis is that it's *you* who's asking the questions, not others. You should not be concerned about "getting it right." The kind of questioning you do in order to develop your ideas should open up possibilities, rather than shutting them down.

Being asked questions makes most people feel put on the spot. If you've done any teaching, you've watched your students dive for cover when you start asking questions. You probably also know from your experience as a student that even at times when you knew the answer, you worried that you had it wrong, or you temporarily forgot it.

So you may need to modify your responses when you actively begin to ask yourself questions. You are in a new position: there is no external audience, and you can try out all sorts of answers; there is no one right answer, and you can even come up with diametrically opposite answers to the same question! Of course, further along you're going to want to get to some answer that feels more or less right, but the best way to do this is to learn to ask questions that may have expansive, divergent answers. For example, "What happens if I argue the opposite of what I've just written down?" "There's something about this piece I've written that's exciting, but disturbing—what is it?" Or even, "What would happen if I ditched this dissertation right now?" Yet another sort, questions you ask yourself from your reader's perspective, can be a useful way of beginning a dialogue with that prospective reader: "Why did you say this here? What do you mean by . . . ? I don't understand." This sort of question can also open up new lines of thought.

A Few Approaches to Writing a First Draft

Choose a work style that suits who you are, not who you'd like to be; do not try to create both a dissertation and a new working style at the same time. I have one writing client who is a very organized person by nature; her tolerance for chaos is low, even though she acknowledges the usefulness of the "make a mess" strategy for getting her ideas down on paper. Jean's solution, when the mess gets to be too much for her and she begins to worry that the forest will never become visible for all the trees, is to generate an outline. She tries to construct the best outline she can at the moment, knowing it's unlikely to be her last. She uses this process as an opportunity to pose important questions to herself: What is this writing really about? Which are my main points, and which are subordinate ones? If I had to say right now what I think is true about this subject, and why, what would I say?

Jean uses making an outline to force herself to ask clarifying and organizing questions. This method works for a person who begins with theory and then moves to the concrete, someone whose thought structure is highly organized; it helps her to rise above the trees/mess/chaos and get to see the forest/order/pattern in what she has written.

But the way you begin to make order out of chaos depends on who you are. If you are by nature orderly and careful, your process may resemble Jean's; if you have, as I do, a greater tolerance for messy writing and operate more intuitively, you may let your freewriting guide you to a gradually emerging clarity. If you're somewhere in between, try alternating freewriting with analytical outlining strategies.

In this essential and anxiety-provoking stage it's very important to remember that you are not going to be able to arrange a personality transplant: if you always work sloppily and intu-itively, don't try for too careful and orderly a process. Trust that the style that's gotten you through projects in the past will do so again, perhaps with some thoughtful retooling. Don't try to turn yourself into someone else.

Similarly, if you are methodical and neat, a New Age or med-itative kind of approach may make you anxious. You might want to modify your careful, cautious approach, but you don't need to turn into a hippy. Your mess may never be as chaotic as the writing of someone of looser temperament. Following are some examples of how people of different sorts manage this stage of writing.

I know a very successful professor and consultant who works in a field that's both scientific and artistic. Carl likes to read, but he prefers to meet the world directly with his eyes: shapes, forms, and images are both his stock-in-trade and his internal organizing principles. On the side, he's not only an avid fisherman, but also a talented artist. But he didn't get to be a tenured full professor at Harvard just by being lively, smart, and artistic; they demanded written work. How does someone whose primary language is not English words but pictures meet such a goal? When I ask him how he thinks one gets from chaos to order, he replies, "I speak my paper into a tape recorder and then have it transcribed. I speak it from the picture I have of it in my head."

When I ask what it is, exactly, that he dictates, he says, "I can *see* the outline, the main ideas." These are often ideas he's worked on for years and given lectures about. He either recon-structs his ideas from "the memory of the slides" he showed at his lectures, or he uses as anchor points for his major papers a series of one- or two-page "idea papers" that he's put together quickly in the past, a series of way stations on the road to the larger work. "And what do you do then, after you've dictated this longer paper and had it typed?" I ask. Carl calls this typescript a "first draft." He says that he then reads and edits, shifting paragraphs, changing vocabulary, and deleting unnecessary parts. About 80 percent of his first draft ends up in the final paper. He is one of those people whose writing goes through several drafts in their heads—in his case, visual rather than verbal drafts—before it ever appears on paper. By the time Carl has a hard copy of his paper, he has his penultimate draft.

Peter, who's in the midst of writing his dissertation, has a different way to get from chaos to draft:

> I don't know whether my procedure for papers will work for chapters, although I suspect it will. Perhaps the word 'procedure' implies more planning and organization than actually gets done. My mess stage generally consists of an assortment of notes jotted down here and there, a pile of books full of stickies, many of which have a few notes jotted down on them, and an array of thoughts floating around in my head. Sometimes I make a rough outline to sort out what to present when. Sometimes I structure my first couple of paragraphs in such a way that they provide a roadmap I use for writing. Sometimes I have an idea in my head of the way the paper should progress. Then I sit down and write. Sometimes what I write follows the outline, but often the outline changes as I progress through the paper. I often use quotations or passages that I am analyzing as moorings for my thoughts. When I am writing I also tend to do a fair amount of in-process sentence-level editing. I know that this 'procedure' would be a recipe for disaster for certain types of writers, but it seems to work for me.

Here is my process, which is at the messy end of the continuum: I generally begin with totally free writing, holding myself only to five pages a day, which can be about anything. Or everything: my cat's sore feet, the week's menus, my offsprings' vacation plans, my reaction to the morning's newspaper, a poem, or the germ of an idea for an essay or a book. This method produces a large number of pages very quickly; very few are useful beyond themselves, but they will ultimately lead me forward into a piece of writing that will take me and itself somewhere, develop into something fit for someone else's eyes. How do I know if I've got anything useful in the midst of the mess? Sometimes it sits right up there and waves at me, or I realize, with a shock, that the line I've just written has potential. I used to leave it to chance to find it again. Now I put a mark in the margin—an arrow, or a note to myself—and in this way increase the chances that I'll remember to use it.

Five pages of handwritten freewriting a day doesn't take very long—somewhere between one and two hours for about 1250 words; sorting and cleaning it up, deciding what's usable and what's to be saved, may take considerably longer. Every so often I read through the past few days' entries, or the past week's, or two weeks' worth. If my freewriting is pouring out, day after day, I don't interrupt it by shifting to the more analytical mode. Sometimes I have a sense of time pressure (wanting to have a draft completed before I go on a vacation, for example) that will move me from freewriting to the next stage. Or I may hit a wall in my writing and decide to deal with it by changing tasks for a while, to see if I can advance on another front (hoping that in rereading I will discover some rough diamonds in what I've already done). As I read the mess I've written, I repeat a few mantras to myself: "It's *supposed* to look like this at this stage," or "Not every single word of this can be garbage."

I will sometimes circle around the same idea or theme more than once, rewriting it without paying particular attention to what I've already written; surprisingly, these iterations move my thoughts forward. My gradually clearer writing reflects my developing thought; my writing is the form in and into which the thought emerges. This iterative development, while a bit fuzzy at first, results in something that looks suspiciously much like a first draft, with a beginning, a middle, an end, and some sense of coherence.

There are as many ways to negotiate this stage in the development of a dissertation as there are dissertation writers. The examples I've given above describe some of the ways that quite diverse people have managed the process. Look at this spectrum to see where you might (or might not) fit; also look at your own style of working, at the ways you've done this step before, at what did or didn't work for you.

You can experiment. Assume that you have created pages and pages of messily written stuff, and now you have very little idea of what to do next. Begin by exploring the mode of organizing your mess that seems most logical to you. Remind yourself that there's got to be something worth using in all of these pages. Then try the scheme that comes first to your mind—*really* try it, allowing your panic to peak and subside, giving it several days, knowing that uneven progress is par for the course. Remind yourself that this is not the first piece of writing you've ever done. Try your old cut-and-paste method (it doesn't matter if it's on the computer or with scissors and tape; it doesn't matter if people laugh, so long as it works).

What if it doesn't work? First ask yourself why not. You may discover that you've taken on too large a job, attempted too much at once, and scared yourself stupid in the process. If so, try the chunking method: "Today I'll just read through the whole mess quickly and mark the things that stand out for me as perhaps not totally dumb. Tomorrow I'll pull them out and see if they have any relation to each other. Wednesday I'll set up some categories to sort them into, and I'll go back and see if there are any other pieces I've overlooked. Thursday I'll take a *very* tentative stab at making an outline."

What if your old revision process, whatever it was, just no longer suits you? Take a look at the various styles described in this chapter and ask yourself if one of those methods might work better for you. If so, try it, continuing to track your own progress to see what works, what doesn't, what might. If cutting and pasting no longer feels right to you, try freewriting, writing about what the problem may be. Write about the chaos, asking yourself all the hard questions knowing that this writing isn't actually going to be part of your dissertation.

What if you discover that you're having not a writing block, but a thinking block? What's the difference between the two? You have a thinking block if you're able to write, but find yourself going around in a seemingly endless series of circles, or if your writing is voluminous but devoid of ideas, or if you do far more writing about trivia and tangents than you do on your dissertation subject. Sometimes you can help yourself through this kind of block by getting tougher, saying, "I can write about any other things for the first five minutes of my writing time, but then I have to hold myself to writing primarily about my subject."

Or consider the possibility of getting a fresh look at your material by having a conversation with your advisor, or with someone else who can understand your topic; isolation sometimes leads to stagnation. Or try writing about what there might be in the knotty place you've reached that's troublesome to you: Do you worry that your advisor won't like it? Or are you uncertain if *you* believe what you've argued? Or is there something in the material itself that disturbs you? It's usually possible to write oneself out of a thinking block. As a final strategy, approach the material again, starting as if you had nothing already written, seeing how fast you can write a really quick version of the chapter. It all came out of your head in the first place, so it's still there, perhaps just needing to be reorganized.

If you haven't created a mess, you may now want to try shaking up your neat work, asking yourself, "Have I left out anything that matters? Do I thoroughly believe what I've written? Are there any nagging questions? Is this the whole story? Have I suppressed my doubts or any contradictory evidence?" This early stage is a very good time to mess up the neatness, for the sake of making sure that your work is as inclusive, as complicated, and as close to the truth of the matter as you can possibly make it.

More Strategies for Working on Your First Draft

Now you're on your way to a complete first draft. Here is my list of specific strategies for making sure you get there.

• Sit down with all your writing, hold your nose, and read through everything you've written several times, looking for different things:
  —Read just for material that stands out as interesting.
  —Read for dominant themes.

- Read for interesting or annoying questions that occur to you as you go through what you've written.
- Read for organizational markers.
- Read in order to organize, marking themes with codes, numbers, letters, or colors.
- Read to extract a provisional outline.
- Read through and put a check in the margin next to anything that's interesting, or seems like it might have potential, or even seems terribly wrong.
- If you find recognizable paragraphs in the mess, try summarizing each of them in a single sentence. This exercise serves several functions: you find out if your paragraph has a central idea, or if it has too many ideas to be covered in a single paragraph; you also produce a collection of sentences that will make it much easier to see the shape of a possible outline.
- If you already have some idea of what approximate categories or themes you're going to develop in your chapter, take out your colored markers, assign a color to each of them, and go through what you've written, color-coding the pieces. If you're working on a word processor, move the pieces you've marked in different colors on your hard copy into different files, rearranging the text to reflect the categories you've defined. You're now well on your way to producing an outline.

These strategies will help you sift through your zero draft as you transform it into a first draft. Add your own inventions as you go along. You'll know when you have a recognizable first draft. It won't necessarily be neat, or elegantly written, or well argued—in fact, it's unlikely to be any of these things—but it will have at least a rudimentary shape and argument, and some interesting, even if incomplete, or mutually contradictory theories. These are the kernels that will develop into the central ideas of your dissertation. Now you're ready to move on to learning how to revise further the draft you hold in your hands.

5

Getting to the Midpoint: Reviewing Your Process and Your Progress

YOU'VE ARRIVED at the midpoint in the dissertation process: depending on how you work, you've written either a first draft of your whole dissertation, or more or less complete versions of about half of your chapters. Your support system is in place. But the clearest indication that you've gotten to this point is that your sense of what it means to write a dissertation has changed. If what worried you most at the outset was "How can I possibly write a book?" you're now asking yourself questions such as "Do I still believe the main argument I've constructed?" and "What *was* it again that made me think I wanted a doctorate?" and "How am I going to arrange my life and work so I'll survive this project?"

Taking Stock of Your Dissertation

Now is the time to review and evaluate where you've come to in your writing and where you have to go, what's working well in the process you're using, and what isn't. This is a good moment to look at your timing and pace, and to think seriously about deadlines. It's also essential to renegotiate how to keep chaos at bay, in your dissertation project and your life, and to reconsider how you can relax and restore yourself for the exciting, but strenuous work ahead

Now that the magnitude of your project has dawned on you, you can assess whether the kinds of planning and organization that you've been using so far are still serving you well. You may feel as if the large quantity of materials and writing you've collected are getting away from you, and you may need to rethink how to keep track of them. And you've probably realized that you have to establish not only the ultimate deadline for completing your dissertation, but also many smaller ones along the way.

Some of you will decide to clean up your act, to work harder than you've been working, in order to meet important deadlines. If you panic because you're not moving along as quickly as you'd planned, and worry that you've fallen into bad habits, you'll resolve to develop a new game plan. But others of you will realize that you have to work *less* hard, that you can't keep up the pace you've been setting for yourself without expiring before you get your degree. You may decide to confront your romantic fantasies of what being a writer means (your life turns out to be nothing like those scenes from old movies about artists), as well as the necessity of taking better care of yourself so that you make it to graduation. When I've heard friends talk about working at writers' retreats like the MacDowell Colony, what I envy most is not that they had all day to work on their projects—that part seems awfully lonely to me—but that lunch was delivered to their cabins in a basket. In the real world, no one delivers your lunch, and you're going to have to make sure you get it anyway.

Soon you will begin to experience a different sort of forward momentum, but not yet. The midpoint in the writing of your dissertation is a time for evaluating your current progress and process, and for making a revised work plan for the future. The two checklists below, and the discussions of them that follow, are meant to help you get started moving again. After that, I'll talk about deadlines, and about rewards and restoring yourself. Look through these checklists and add to them any items you think I've missed. Use them periodically during this middle part of the dissertation process to see how you're doing, and to stay in charge of your life and your work. Time spent evaluating your writing process and progress will more than repay itself.

Your Writing Process

Here are some useful questions to ask yourself:

___ How do you feel about the writing process you're using?
___ Do you feel that your process is doing what you need it to do?
___ Are you writing regularly, with reasonable ease?
___ Are you able to focus clearly on your writing?
___ Is the place you've chosen to write working well for you?
___ Are you reading too much? enough?
___ Are you using other people well?
___ How are you and your advisor getting along?
___ Are you letting too many things get in the way of your writing?
___ Are you well enough organized so you can get your work done without having to step over either psychological or literal obstacles?
___ Is the process you've set up efficient?

Very few people are so self-punishing that they can continue to engage in a process that's painful and awkward, or in a regimen that makes them feel incompetent. If you're only managing to write late at night once or twice a week and one morning on the weekend; if you don't have any place (even if it's a broom closet) to call your own for your writing; if you've set up your schedule so that you always have to justify the time you spend writing to someone else—be that your partner, your child, or your boss; or if you have to steal moments while the baby or everyone else in the house sleeps, it *might* be possible to write a dissertation, but I wouldn't lay odds on it. Even if you succeed, it will be a miserable experience. I've known people in extreme circumstances who really had no good alternatives, but most people do have some choices.

If your examination of your writing process reveals nightmare conditions like the ones described above, you need to ask yourself why you're setting yourself up to fail. Or if your circumstances are the result of just not having thought about what you were doing, start thinking now and make some changes: Find a place to write that works for you (if your house won't work, go out to the library, or to a friend's house that's empty during the day). Establish more work time, even if that means taking a part-time leave from work or hiring more babysitters. Given how much your degree has probably cost you already, the costs of making the dissertation process more workable are not substantial—particularly since they will allow you to finish. Remember that you are entitled to put your dissertation first (not for seven years, but for a while). Realize that it's time you stopped asking other people's permission to do so.

About you and your advisor: Is it time for the two of you to talk about your work together and perhaps to retool some aspects of it (the frequency of your meetings, the kinds of comments you're receiving), or to look at difficulties either of you is having with your current arrangements?

Some thoughts on focusing, and on enjoying yourself: Some days you'll be sleepy, and no one ever said every moment of writing a dissertation was fun; but if every day is sleepy, and it's never fun to work on your dissertation, you really have to ask yourself why. If you can't answer that question, get help from friends, or your advisor, or a professional. Every once in a while someone with these symptoms is trying to tell herself that she no longer wants a doctorate. Perhaps she's been doing it for someone else; perhaps her interests have changed. But most of the time your reasons will be less earthshaking: you've neglected yourself by not sleeping, or you've been grandiose in your estimate of how many other different jobs you could do while writing your dissertation. Or you're being too generous, or too masochistic, and are letting other people distract you.

Other people: Many of us have an impossible person (or two or three) in our lives whom we fantasize about getting rid of. This is usually not possible, because we're (a) related to them closely by blood, or (b) love them, or (c) would feel too guilty about doing it. If there is a person in your life who leaves you upset and unable to think about your own stuff for hours or days after each encounter, now is the time to take a vacation from that person. You can even tell him/her so explicitly: "I'm going to be a recluse for the next several weeks while I work on my dissertation. I'll call you when I come up for air. Don't call me. I'll be unfit for human companionship."

I wouldn't advise that you give up human society. I am suggesting, though, that you become selectively antisocial: that you either have no phone in your thesis room or that you don't pick it up when it rings. (If you are one of the last people in America without an answering machine, now is the time to buy one, so that you're not cutting yourself off permanently from other people, just postponing conversations to a time when they won't interfere with your work.) Someone has noted that as a working parent you only get to do two out of the following three things well: work, be a parent, and have a social life. Whether or not you have children, if you're going to finish your degree, you'll find that you have to be a bit ruthless about whom you make time for, and when you do so. One of the tests of a partner you want to keep for life is that he can understand that your dissertation is your top priority—not forever, but for now. This is a good time to work hard to diminish the pain in your life, particularly that which comes from acquaintances who leave you feeling drained or disturbed after you've hung out with them for a while. Learning how to stop feeding people who bite the hand that feeds them is a good lesson for life, as well as for your dissertation year.

If you don't live alone, review with your partner/kids/room-mates how life is working for all of you, and hash out the diffi-culties. They may be tired of your piled-up papers on the dining room table. You have probably discovered that you can't party late with them and still be able to write the next morning. Babysitting hours may be insufficient. . . . Don't just suffer, *do something* about what isn't working.

Although other people are often the most potent distractors from your work, chaos around you, of whatever sort, and the failure to organize your work, both theoretically and concretely, can also be hurdles to getting to your dissertation. Each of us has a different level of tolerance for clutter and dirt—my own is not particularly high—but the important question to ask yourself is whether the atmosphere in which you're trying to work is preventing you from working. Do you spend a lot of time hunting for papers or diskettes? Is your personal life the kind of disaster that engenders middle-of-the-night crises that leave you wiped out the next day, unable to work? Do you find yourself not sure whether you've already written a particular section? Have you missed important institutional deadlines, like filing the papers necessary for getting your degree? Even free spirits have to make themselves more organized (at least temporarily) for the sake of not getting in their own way during this complex process.

Keep chaos at bay. It's one thing to keep track of fifty pages or two computer files, but quite another to track five or even ten times that much material. Review your systems: for backing up files, for saving papers in ways that permit easy retrieval, for keeping the clutter on our desk down to a level where you can work, for keeping your surroundings clean enough so that you don't get either roaches or trench mouth. If you can't do these things for yourself, ask the most compulsive friend you have to help you—to get your papers organized, to turn off the phone, or to get you to make a careful list of what you've written and what's left to write. And if all other methods fail, hire a therapist to help you figure out why you let self-generated chaos get in the way of your succeeding in your life.

Spend some time looking at your work process: at how much time you're spending on your dissertation and when, at exactly how you're writing. (Are you trying for a final draft each time you sit down? Is it working?) Look at whether the process feels efficient. Particularly examine how much you're reading. It's more common for the students I've worked with to read too much than to read too little. They use reading as a distraction, or as a way to avoid having to think their own thoughts, or as a magic charm: "If I read *everything* in the field, *then* I'll be able to write and be sure I haven't missed *anything*." Relax. You're sure to miss something, and it's very unlikely to matter much. It may make you fell very rigorous and virtuous to have read every article ever published on your topic, as well as related ones, but it won't help you finish your dissertation. Bite the bullet and get back to your own writing, and your own thinking.

If other parts of your writing process feel awkward, or inefficient, look at them hard and, once again, ask yourself some questions: Why is writing this section so hard? Is there something about the way I'm organizing this argument that isn't working? What would happen if, in revising, I tried x instead of y? If you can't begin to answer, once again, ask other people to help you. Your advisor and other students can be good sources of suggestions. Don't be afraid to experiment; you might be surprised to find that alternative strategies can change your angle of approach to your dissertation, allowing you to get more done and to derive more pleasure from the work.

Your Writing Progress

Here are some useful questions to ask yourself about the pace and timing of your dissertation work:

____Are you moving forward? Do you sometimes feel as if you're going in circles? Do you know when? why?

____Is your pace accelerating? decelerating? If it's steady, does it feel like the right pace?

____What speeds you up? What slows you down?

____Is your pace one that you can maintain over time?

____Is it a pace that will allow you to finish on time?

—— Are you undoing as much writing as you're producing? If so, why?

—— Do you know roughly how much you can write in a certain period of time?

—— Have you thought about, and discussed with your advisor, how large your project must be, how small it can be and still be acceptable, and how long you have? That is, have you calibrated the process?

—— Have you made a tentative timetable?

Most of these questions are addressed in my discussion of deadlines later in this chapter, but there are a few I'd like to talk about now. A few years ago I had a student who worked, and worked, and worked, providing me along the way with every single draft she produced; the problem was, they were nearly identical. She was one of the casualties of the computer-assisted dissertation: at times when she really didn't have any new ideas, she'd bring the file of a chapter up on her computer and fiddle around with paragraphs, moving them up and down and so forth. You get the idea. Although she eventually finished, and wrote a good dissertation, she used a very inefficient process, and she ended up doing too much work even for the fine piece she managed to produce. (She also provided me with scrap paper sufficient for the next few years.)

I have named a more extreme version of this problem "the Penelope Syndrome." Penelope, you probably remember, spent the days of Odysseus's absence weaving and the nights unweaving in order to hold off the suitors who were harassing her. For a multitude of other reasons, some dissertation writers act like Penelope: they write a few decent paragraphs, and then a day or a week later they decide that what they have written is not any good at all, and they toss it. They do this over, and over, and over again, so that the stack of completed pages remains exactly the same height over time. If you're doing this, you may be overly perfectionistic, or maybe you have a screwy idea of how one writes, or, on some deeper level, you may be very conflicted over finishing your degree. If you recognize yourself as a Penelope type, try forcing yourself to move forward. *Even if you think what you've written is garbage,* don't erase or throw anything out. Ask someone else to help you look it over later and make some suggestions for revision. If you can't stop undoing your work, consider your university's counselling center as your next stop.

The question of how long a dissertation is long enough is easy to answer: the shortest one your committee will accept. You might want to write the final word on your subject, but tell yourself that finishing the dissertation is only the first step toward this goal, and that not putting everything in your thesis will leave you other papers and books to write after you've gotten your degree and an academic position. One of the most common problems encountered among the students I counsel is biting off too large a topic or question for their dissertation. Don't feel like you're cheating or slacking off if you end up reducing the size of your project. Instead, take it as evidence that you are thinking hard and being selective.

On Deadlines

I recently suggested to a friend who is working on his Ph.D. that he add to his vita, in the section that describes his thesis, a line that reads "Estimated date of completion . . . " and includes his best guess of what that date will be. This is the sort of act that strikes terror in the hearts of most graduate students, and for good reason.

The word "deadline" itself can chill your blood—I braced myself before I looked up its origins. Even the more benign of the two definitions given in the *Oxford English Dictionary* suggests why. The first definition comes from the language of fishing: "A line that does not move or run"—so much for our fantasies of moveable deadlines! The second is much worse: "A line drawn around a military prison, beyond which a prisoner is liable to be shot down." For most of us the resonance of the word "deadline" is, "Meet it or you're dead meat."

External deadlines have unfortunate associations, starting with our earliest reactions to "Hurry up and put on your shoes, or you'll be late for school." Neither kids nor adults like the feeling that someone else is controlling their lives. Some of us get anxious in the face of adult deadlines and suddenly shrink to child size, with a child's feelings of inadequacy, sure we can't possibly meet the demands. Some of us get stubborn, digging in our heels and refusing to budge, much as we did at age three, four, or five. Some of us get desolate and want to give up before we've even tried, sure that meeting deadlines is out of the question.

Because deadlines are an essential, and at times a very frightening, part of the dissertation process, much of my work consulting to graduate students is about deadlines. I often see people who are having terrible trouble meeting them, who are so frightened that they can't either face them or make them; or they are so frightened that they have, by the time they come to see me, missed one or more important ones. How can you learn to use deadlines to empower yourself, and exert control over the dissertation process, rather than to scare yourself into paralysis? Establishing your own work deadlines can be a wonderful way of taking back ownership of time for yourself in this process. What you need to do for this to happen is to consider carefully the possible differences between external deadlines (those set by your advisor, or department, or university) and internal or personal deadlines, those you set for yourself.

Deadlines set by external authorities can seem to have nothing to do with your needs or with the way you work; you may feel like someone else is just telling you what to do. You may make the mistake of reenacting this struggle in the deadlines you set for yourself, but you don't have to. Follow B. F. Skinner's wise advice: don't set goals for yourself that you can't meet, because you will gradually wipe out ("extinguish," Skinner would say) the behavior, in this case the writing, that you thought you were trying to encourage. Setting yourself up to fall on your face, over and over again, is *not* a way to encourage yourself. Whatever your own history with deadlines, learning how to set them for yourself can permanently change the way you work, if you make such changes in a thoughtful and sensible way.

Particularly at the outset, the deadlines you set for yourself need to be very, very generous ones. If you think it will take you two weeks to finish the next chapter, give yourself three. If you finish early, you'll feel particularly fine. Most important is that you finish the chapter and give yourself cause for celebration, rather than disappointment.

Begin by experimenting with different sorts of deadlines, trying to think about times when you've met goals in the past, and what the circumstances of those projects were. Was the person who set the goals on your side? Were the projects collaborative efforts? Was the work something you were enthusiastic about? Were the goals generous and realistic ones?

Some of us begin this shift by making our own deadlines as

punitive as the external ones feel to us, and sometimes even more stringent (to prove we're really serious, in the hopes of forcing more work out of ourselves, or maybe we're driven by internal demons and want to relive our own history). This trip is not necessary. Set up deadlines so they involve rewards, not punishments. Do not set them up so that you have to be superhuman to meet them. Perhaps you can work nonstop for a few days, but no one can sustain that sort of effort over the long haul. As you begin your experiment, set very easy goals. Every one that you meet will empower you, so that you can make the next hurdle a bit more strenuous. This is the way to turn "I think I can" into "I know I can." Make the working conditions that you set up for yourself benevolent.

On chunking: Perhaps the most terrifying of all deadlines is the one for a whole project: "Your dissertation is due exactly a year from yesterday." Faced with this sort of statement, very few of us are any good at imagining how to get from here to there. What you need to do is to break up that single deadline into a series of much smaller ones, each of which you can imagine meeting. With a dissertation, these smaller goals and time frames can be stated in terms of a certain number of pages, or chapters, or sections of chapters. Your fundamental task is to divide the single project into pieces small enough so that, one by one, they don't frighten you: to get to a place where you can say, "O.K., I can do that much."

What if you miss a deadline? Follow the rule for what to do if you fall off a horse: get right back on. Make a new, easy, realistic deadline, and get back to work. Don't waste time crying over lost opportunities, take advantage of new ones.

Sprinting for short stretches is fine, and sometimes very productive, but you can't sprint for a whole marathon, and that is what a dissertation is. Consider using close-up markers—"By the time the kids get out of school," "By Christmas vacation," "By this Friday"—and then make a determined run for them. And when you meet them, be sure to reward yourself.

Pay close attention to who you are, not who you might like to be. By now you've had enough life experience to know how much pressure you can stand: how much helps you produce, and how much is too much and scares you stupid or exhausts you so that you stop working. You need to create work strategies that are useful for you.

Some folks are so turned off by *any* sense of being controlled—*even by themselves*—that they rebel against even their own deadlines. If you're one of these people, you have a big problem that could keep you from finishing your degree. If it's really bad, get professional help. If it's intermittent, think hard and listen to your feelings in answer to the question, "Whose dissertation is this, anyway?" Watch out for this sort of resurgent stubbornness and stalling: remember that you were the one who set these goals, and you did so for a reason.

Perhaps it's not such a bad thing after all that my friend has to say something on his vita about his estimated date for completing his degree. Deadlines, although scary, can also be opportunities for remembering who owns your dissertation, for trying on the idea of finishing your degree, and, perhaps most important, for taking back ownership of both your writing and your time.

R&R

No one can be totally self-denying for as long as it takes to write a dissertation. There are different sorts of rest and rewards that you need to consider. The first of these is ongoing support for your enterprise in the form of household help (hired, bartered, or given to you out of love) with cooking, cleaning, childcare, and laundry. Absolutely essential is tech support— computer, research, editing, and secretarial. Both you and your project are worth help, and you deserve it, if you can possibly arrange it. And it needn't break the bank; if necessary you can practice the Rapunzel strategy (mortage your firstborn child, book, or winning lottery ticket so long as it buys you help). Living in a community with other grad students or academics who are likely to understand these needs should make getting help easier. Just as you probably decided that a computer was a necessary investment in your professional future, you need to decide (particularly, but not only, if you have kids) that some outlay of money for decent take-out food, occasional cleaning help, or someone who will save you precious time by tracking down footnotes for you or installing the new software in your computer and teaching you how to use it, is an important investment in this project, and in yourself. If it makes you calmer and less stressed, you will finish sooner. If you finish sooner, you'll earn an income sooner. I rest my case.

Rewards for meeting specific deadlines, or for just plain working hard are also important: You may not like M&M's, but there's probably something else you really like, whether it's food, or Pink Panther movies, or a trip to the local aquarium, or evenings spent with friends. Make sure that you mark and celebrate the times when you meet important (and even not-so-important) goals by treating yourself to your favorite rewards. Doing so will make it even more likely that you'll meet your next goal.

Build into your workweek times when you can relax and times when you can undo the tension that comes from spending hours each day sitting still and concentrating hard. Go for a walk or a run. Go to the gym and work out or swim. Get a massage. Do yoga or meditate. Work in the garden. Set up a weekly supper date with good friends. Make sure you have at hand a book you want to read, or a CD you want to hear, when you're ready for downtime. To brighten up my work environment I have a succession of indoor bulbs flowering next to my desk, and when my fig tree comes out of its annual hibernation I keep it in the sunny window in my study, where I can watch leaf after leaf unfurl, and be inspired to grow my writing.

This is the time for stashing in your cupboards the tea you most love, for putting in your freezer the shrimp that go into your favorite quick supper. Don't skimp on good food; what you spend on it will repay you in energy, health, and good spirits. (Do you know that greasy food will make you sleepy? Don't subject yourself to a steady diet of junk food. If cooking is one of your pleasures, spend some of your weekend time preparing foods that will sustain you during the week.) And although a glass of wine at dinner may give you pleasure and relax you, drinking too much alcohol or using other drugs can ruin your sleep and your health, and it will certainly not improve your intellectual performance (the myth of the famous writer-as-lush notwithstanding). Indulge in take-out food and a video every Tuesday night (pizza is cheap, and most libraries loan videos), a long walk several times a week, or a concert series (most universities have free or very inexpensive concerts that will fit into even a grad student's budget). You can't afford not to provide yourself with such treats.

Many of the dissertation writers I've worked with have had ongoing health problems. For some this has been the result of living with small children (who are notorious agents of contagion) or of bad luck. For others, I'm pretty sure they've been sicker than they might have been had they been "selfish" enough (that's what they'd call it, not I) to take decent care of themselves by getting enough sleep, eating well, exercising, and managing to get enough help. Ongoing, unremitting stress is not good for either the soul or the immune system. So call it "self-ishness" if you will, but vow to take extra good care of yourself. I call it an investment in your finishing your degree expeditiously and well—in both senses of that word.

• • •

By the time you've worked your way through the middle passage of the dissertation process, following my suggestions thus far, you will be wiser and more experienced as a writer. If you're also tired, you'll have developed some good ways to restore yourself. And you will have a firmer, clearer knowledge that you are in charge of the progress and quality of your dissertation, and that, for better and worse, it belongs to you.

6

Interruptions from Outside and Inside

THIS CHAPTER is about the many events, both internal and external, that can interrupt your writing. Whether or not they actually are, these occurrences often feel beyond your control. Emergencies, interruptions by others, and acts of God are external. I'll talk about how to reestablish control in some of these circumstances, while acknowledging that others are beyond your control. Then I'll move on to inside interruptions—ambivalence, static, and writing scared—those ways in which, for whatever reasons, you get in your own way.

Interruptions from Outside

In a useful and funny essay called "Still Just Writing," the novelist Anne Tyler describes a variety of interruptions to her writing life that result from having children, pets, and relatives; that is, from having a life besides her writing. It turns out that even if you've taken the advice I offered in chapter 1 of this book, time and chance happen to us all: the odds are very good that you will be unexpectedly interrupted by outside persons and occasions at some crucial moments during your dissertation.

These interruptions can range from the trivial (a cold that clogs your brain as well as your nose for a few days) to the catastrophic (a serious illness of your own, or the death of someone close to you). I've heard of every sort of event imaginable in between these extremes. Hard disks failing, for instance—and here I must offer this advice in advance of any other: KEEP A HARD COPY OF EVERY VERSION OF YOUR THESIS. You can make up for squandering paper by reusing all the drafts as scrap paper for the rest of your life. In addition to computer maladies, thesis writers can have recurrent sinus infections (it's really hard to write with a splitting headache), abusive spouses, and catastrophes in housing or with automobiles. Of course, the risks are increased by graduate students' tendency to live at the economic edge: new cars and attentive landlords are rare in this population.

I've worked with people who, while writing their dissertations, have suffered serious illnesses, or someone dear to them has been ill, or someone close to them has died (this particular event usually takes a lot of energy and time to recover from, and if you don't take the time when it happens, the repercussions are likely to take it from you later). I've known others who have had to change jobs in the middle of writing a dissertation, and I've worked with several women clients who were simultaneously occupied not only with their theses, but also with pregnancy and birth. (I've been in the position of telling a graduate student who was eight and a half months pregnant with her second child that this was no excuse for not finishing her dissertation. She finished, but I developed quite a reputation among her fellow students!) If you have any choice, there are changes in your external life *not* to make while you're writing a dissertation:

Don't move, unless you've just been evicted. Don't renovate. Don't get a puppy.

I've dealt with students whose advisors went away on sabbatical for the crucial year when the students were writing their dissertations (see my advice on this subject in chapter 2), and also some whose advisors got terribly ill or died. All of which is to say, life goes on in the course of the significant length of time it takes to write a dissertation, and things happen. Some of them can be awful things over which you have absolutely no control. What do you do in the face of this fact?

You wouldn't have gotten this far in your graduate study if you didn't have some resilience and some capacity to control your own life. Paradoxically, though, some major events require the opposite of control: acknowledging your helplessness and letting go of the illusion that you can have an effect on what's happening. Trying to control the uncontrollable is a terrible, and painful, waste of time and energy. Similarly, indulging in guilt ("If I'd paid more attention, John wouldn't have gotten ill"), or shame ("I *should* have been able to do something about this") wastes the energy you need to deal with dreadful events. You're probably also going to have to get through your anger at life having dealt you such a nasty blow. It's hard not to take such blows personally, particularly if this is the one time in your life when you've decided to devote yourself to your own project.

Here are some things you *can* do about events that are beyond your control:

• Make a plan that deals with the reality, with what you can and can't do about the situation.

• Ask yourself, "Is this a matter of professional life and death? Does this mean I'll *never* finish my dissertation, or only that I'll finish it later than I would have liked?"

• Consider the "act of God" explanation: this is one useful way to remind yourself that some things just happen. Some things come from a source—call it what you will—over which you have absolutely no control.

• Work to understand and explore your life priorities, and get them very clear. Under some circumstances, there are things that are even more important than finishing a dissertation.

• Know that although a few people in this world are able to find solace in writing or working during catastrophic times, they are very rare.

• Learn the difference between what's flexible and what isn't—what you can change, and what you can't—and don't waste your energy struggling with what you can't change.

• Talk to the powers that be in your department and university. They have lives, too, and most will respond to your catastrophes with flexibility and decency.

• Try not to add panic to the mess.

• Give yourself leeway, and get help. Get lots of help, whether it's with finishing the editing of your dissertation, if you're at that stage, or with formatting it, or with keeping your household running, or with taking care of the kids. And get help with your feelings if you are overwhelmed: if your body is showing signs of emotional stress, or you're having ongoing trouble sleeping, or you're feeling depressed, or scarily wired, or out of touch. Talk with your friends, talk with your doctor, talk with a therapist, but don't try to get through this time of crisis alone.

• Don't waste your time indulging in wishful thinking, in the "if onlys."

Ambiguous Interruptions and Events

We need to distinguish between interruptions that are acts of God—there is no way you could have prevented them, and not much you can do about them—and those that are in some way or other the result of your own actions. For example, nearly missing my own Ph.D. qualifying exams because of a threatened miscarriage, while technically the result of my own action, would probably qualify as an act of God. But the many other roadblocks that I installed quite unconsciously—working in the wrong place, allowing myself to be distracted by friends, not getting enough sleep, and not exploring my deep, ongoing ambivalence about getting a Ph.D.—would not.

Some people operate right on the boundary between external and internal interruptions far more often than they consciously know. Sometimes awful things happen to them through absolutely no fault of their own; sometimes, though, they invite chaos into their lives. They may be overly involved with their students and their relatives; they may work on behalf of others as if they were Dorothy Day or Mother Theresa (which is fine, but not while working on a dissertation). They may, quite unconsciously, seek distractions from writing.

Cultivate ruthlessness (which is not the same as irresponsibility or cruelty) while writing a dissertation. If you're planning on finishing your degree, you have to focus on your own work, at times to the exclusion of the rest of the world. (This is often harder for women to do than for men.) Here's a useful mind game: tell yourself that the increased credibility you will gain from having the Ph.D. after your name will make you a better helper of those who need you.

What else is in this category of not quite acts of God? Giving away your time. Not allowing for the possibility that you'll catch the flu or that your computer will break down. Pretending that life is ordinary when you schedule vacations or social obligations. This is not the year to be president of the PTA, not the year to have the family holiday party at your house, nor to be secretary of the dog training club. This is the time for saying no, *guiltlessly,* to any obligations that aren't absolutely necessary, and to anyone who thinks she has a lien on your time. If you are prone to take on such obligations, you'll do more than your share in your lifetime, so you can excuse yourself during this dissertation-writing year.

Engage those who care about you, and, thus, about your finishing this project, on the side of your being ruthless. For example, if you're already teaching, ask your chair to remind you not to take on any extra committee assignments; ask your parent (real or imagined) to give you permission to have a messy apartment, or an overgrown yard (or to come and mow the lawn). Ask your friends to remind you that when someone asks for a chunk of your time, you are free to say no immediately; if you're tempted to answer yes, though, learn to say instead, "I'll have to think about it and get back to you." And then do think about it, hard, and then think about how much you want and need to finish your dissertation. The only reason for saying yes to others' requests for your time is that there is an overwhelming reason for doing so. Don't use other people's needs as a way of acting out your ambivalence about completing your thesis.

Watch out for your unconscious, paradoxical though that may sound: learn to recognize the signs that you're postponing work, or not feeling entitled to finish your degree.

And if your dissertation has been interrupted by some major external event, read Anne Tyler's essay. It will give you a laugh and some solace, and remind you that life, and writing, go on.

Interruptions from Inside

In this section I'll describe three kinds of mental tricks we play on ourselves that can interrupt progress on dissertations. The first is ambivalence, the second, mental static, and the third, anxiety—what I'll call "writing scared."

Ambivalence

Part of you really wants to finish, and part of you may not, and the latter part is likely to be sneaky ("Wouldn't this be the perfect time, when I have no other outside obligations, to have my wisdom teeth/appendix/hernia fixed?" "While I'm home anyway, I could take care of a puppy."). Because writing a dissertation is so often lonely work, the part of you that is social, that likes and needs companionship, will continually try to drag you out into company—or drag it in.

Ambivalence always calls up a playground image for me: a seesaw with two kids of about equal weight and force who try to keep the board level. What happens to those kids is relevant here: they just sit there, *and nothing happens,* except for a lot of tension. This is a lot like the more complex internal playground on which you play out the questions of wanting, or not wanting, to write a dissertation. "What do you mean?" you might ask. "I don't want to write my dissertation? Look at how hard I've been working, how many sacrifices I've made in order to work on this project!"

There is no inherent contradiction between that statement and your being ambivalent. It is absolutely possible to want very much to write your dissertation, and *also* to want very much not to—and if the forces are just about equal, you will end up in the seesaw position with a lot of tension and no motion. One solution to this problem is to recognize it and then push off from the ground again; another is to consider applying force as well as weight. In the latter case that might mean engaging a friend as a cheering squad, or asking your advisor to set you frequent deadlines, or listing explicitly for yourself all the reasons it would be lovely to be finished with your degree.

Most of us are ambivalent about the important psychic events of our lives: getting married, having children, being in love, or taking the sort of major leap forward professionally that earning a doctorate constitutes. You can't banish mixed feelings by denying them, or trying to legislate them out of existence, but if you pay attention to them, they may then let you move forward. William G. Perry Jr. once wrote an essay called "Sharing in the Costs of Growth," in which he talks about how much loss and grief is involved in any change, *even change for the better.* Believe it. Learn to recognize, feel, laugh at, your own ambivalence, and then to get on with your work.

Static
Static is my name for the unrelated thoughts, feelings, and other distractions that pass through your mind while you're writing or trying to write; it is the mental debris that seems to have little to do with what you're writing about. When you read novels and are supposedly inside a character's mind, what you usually see is

a neat, single line of thought (Joyce's *Ulysses* is one of the wonderful exceptions). If fictional characters aren't always strictly logical, their thoughts nearly always seem to be connected; you follow them with more or less ease, as you're meant to. Real thought, though, is much more complicated and chaotic: You may simultaneously consider an abstract idea, remember what you forgot to do before coming to the library, and notice that you're hungry. Even when you are writing about something that is terribly important to you, your thoughts may frequently wander down many side paths.

Struggling writers complain about getting easily distracted and note that distractions seem more often to come from the inside than from the outside. They tend to speak about this static in moralistic terms: "I shouldn't be letting my mind wander like this," or "I've got to concentrate better so I can ignore the distractions." They experience static as disruptive, disorderly, and dismaying, a sign of incipient brain rot. There is an interesting experiment you can try with your own static that may convince you otherwise: instead of trying to push it out of your mind, try writing down whatever is in your head. If you do this over time, you may be surprised to discover that there is indeed a method to your seeming madness: themes that are present in what seemed to be chaos, themes that reappear over and over again.

One very common theme of static concerns unfulfilled obligations, real or imaginary: "I need to call my elderly aunt, *right now*," or "I probably ought to be cooking tonight, since my partner has cooked for the whole week," or "This house looks like a pigsty. I should really take some time off to clean it up." Some of these thoughts may be about the real toll that writing takes on other parts of your life: you have to lower your housekeeping standards, make fewer phone calls, do less than your share of the household upkeep for a while. But some of the static is about a much deeper part of being a writer: there is something inherently and wonderfully selfish about claiming time for one's own thoughts and words, about taking them seriously enough to dedicate a major piece of your life to them, and a smaller piece to the needs of others. I've written about this in an essay called "A Room of One's Own Is Not Enough": "The worry that the creative act of writing, or speaking out, will rupture connectedness is not a fantasy. From the inside we know that our own strong feelings may do just that. We worry that our 'selfishness' will be met with hostility from those we care about." It's easier to deal with feelings of "selfishness" if you acknowledge them to yourself.

So static can come from many different causes: it may be merely the way our minds work; it may represent internal conflict about being a writer; it may be a defensive maneuver that we employ when we're conflicted about our accomplishment or afraid that our speaking out will hurt someone else. At its worst, it may be present in order to keep us from writing at all.

There are two different ways to deal with static, and either one can work. Try them out in turn, and see which works better for you. The first is what I call the Buddhist way, and it is based on meditation techniques, what has been described as "training the mind-puppy not to wander off." There are various focusing techniques you can use to return your attention to your subject, not so much pushing the static out of your mind as pulling your thoughts back to the topic at hand. These techniques can be found in any of a number of fine books on meditation and mindfulness.

What I want to describe in greater detail is the second type of strategy, which may sound paradoxical: it encourages you to move toward static, rather than away from it. Try keeping a separate pad next to your main work and just jotting down the static as it happens. Or actually include it in your main text, with brackets around it (or, if you're writing by hand, use a different color ink). If your head is going in several different directions at once (say you're trying to write, make a grocery shopping list, and plan a wedding), keep separate pads for each. Giving the static a little bit of your time may keep it from taking all of your time and breaking your concentration.

You can try this sneaky trick, one of my daughter's favorites from her year of dissertation writing: keep a running list of all the other things you'd like to jump up and do (wash the bathroom, practice your violin, pay the bills, clean your desk . . .), and then promise yourself that you can do any or all of them, *as soon as you've finished your set number of pages for the day.* You'll be amazed how much less attractive the items on your list look once you've finished your writing that day!

There is one particularly insidious form of static that you ought to know about, what I call "thinking about, rather than thinking in, your dissertation." Static like this often takes the form of fantasies about what other folks have said about your topic, or questions about how brilliant or foolish your finished work is going to look to others, or worry about whether or not you've really chosen the right subject. These meta-thoughts that *seem* to be about your dissertation tend to be repetitious, persistent, and preoccupying, and their ultimate effect is to keep you disengaged from, and uncommitted to, your work. If static seems to break your train of thought repeatedly in this or some other way, you might first try writing for yourself about why you seem so unable to move your dissertation ahead. If your distractibility is constant and incapacitating, try getting professional help to deal with it; you may be struggling with unconscious forces that will not allow you to write until you have recognized and dealt with them.

Writing Scared

It's a rare dissertation writer who is never really scared about his project. Writing a dissertation provides the perfect medium for anxiety, for both healthy and neurotic reasons. It's a big deal to write a book, both psychologically and realistically. Serious writing can have lots of meanings: "I have something important to say," or "I've finally found my own voice," or "I have chutzpah, and that's O.K.," or "I can finally risk going for something I really want."

There are many reasons for thesis writers to become discouraged. You may be surrounded by friends or family who don't understand what you're doing, and don't support you in it. Writing a dissertation takes a long time, despite the aberrant person everyone knows about who cranked out a thesis in a few months. It takes an enormous amount of hopefulness and a large capacity for persistence and focus, some of which you may have to develop as you go along. Difficult or unsupportive advisors are not as rare as they should be. And bad work habits tend to get magnified in a project of this size.

There are many internal reasons why thesis writers get scared. I'm not going to linger on them, because they tend to be very individual. You will either find a way to help yourself out of this place, or get friends or teachers to help you out of it or enable you to endure it. And if it's really driving you nuts and keeping you from getting any work done, you can get professional help. Universities sometimes employ people who specialize in writing blocks, either within their health services or their academic support services. Ask whether your institution does. If it doesn't, and you are still seriously frightened, find outside help.

This story may be enlightening: Years ago, shortly after a colleague and I had begun a writing center, we put up on every Harvard University bulletin board we could find a poster advertising my workshop, called "Writing Scared." I'd never taught such a workshop before, and suddenly I was seized by waves of panic over whether I'd be able to do it. Knowing I needed help, I went to visit a man who had been my teacher in a counselling course. I told him how anxious I was that "I'd promised to unscare any writer who was blocked, anywhere in the whole university," and that I didn't know how I was going to do it. He offered me a very simple and immensely relieving answer: "You haven't offered that. You've only promised to help them write *even though they're scared.*"

If you're a scared writer, one moral of this story is that it's perfectly possible to write scared. You don't have to get "unscared" first; you just need to learn how to work despite your anxiety. In fact, writing is probably the world's best cure for a scared writer. It is unnecessary to get completely over your fright about writing before you begin; it isn't even necessary to get over it before you finish. It is useful to respect your fright (but not too much), to listen to it, to investigate it, all as part of coming to know yourself as a writer, that is, as someone who writes.

You can ask yourself what scares you so much; try writing down the answer, and pay attention to what you've written. You can pretend you're giving advice to one of the students you may have met when you were a teaching assistant, or to your fellow students who've told you about their blocks. You can try mantras for inspiration, magic charms to keep away the evil writing spirits, and rewards for times when you write through your block. You can write a letter to your "watcher." Being scared is sometimes a defense, a wonderful way of shifting your deep concern about the meaning of what it is you're trying to accomplish to a symptom that keeps you from doing it. But there are good ways to keep the fear from getting the best of you.

Funky Exercises for Times When You're Stuck

Anyone who writes seriously over any period of time is likely to experience times when writing is difficult, when you feel like you're slogging through molasses, when even you are bored by what you're writing, or, even worse, times when you just can't write at all. What do you do then? The temptation is to give it up and do something else: go to the movies, go to the beach, go on vacation, or move to the other side of the continent. Sometimes one of these strategies helps: a weekend off when you're exhausted or disheartened can begin to refill the dry well. But sometimes running away from your writing is exactly the wrong fix for the problem, and it may even be harmful; and sometimes— say when you have an absolute deadline to meet—it's just not possible, unless you want to give up your writing project altogether. (Tempting as this may seem at times, don't give in to this course of action unless you've considered it *very* carefully, looked at it over time and in different lights, and talked it over with rational people who have your best interests at heart.) So what else can you do? What you can do involves writing, but a different sort than what you're stuck on. The general rule is, writing is writing, and if you can't write your dissertation, just continue writing—anything—to keep your muscles in shape, and to keep yourself from getting phobic. At times when you feel like you can't write, the strategy is to *keep writing*.

Try limiting your writing time drastically. This is a severe strategy appropriate to a desperate situation, but it can really work. Say to yourself, "I am only allowed to write for half an hour (or whatever seems to you much too short a time), and no more than that." Pick a length of time—it can be as little as ten minutes a day—*that you are absolutely certain you can manage*. The aim of this particular tactic is not to go on writing for only this short amount of time every day indefinitely, because you probably won't ever finish your dissertation if you do; the aim is to get back to a place where it's once again comfortable and, most important, possible, to write.

Write in some other form. If you've always aspired to be a poet, this is your chance: try haiku, try two-syllable lines in a syllabic poem. Write dialogue. Write E-mail or a letter to someone (real, imaginary, or yourself) about your dissertation. (And then save a copy.) Write anything, because writing is writing.

Apply the principle that says "No dessert until you finish your zucchini." Pick something you *really* want to do, the thing without which your day feels incomplete (taking a shower, unless, of course, that's the way you get your eyes open in the morning; reading the newspaper; having a cappuccino from the café downtown; taking a walk in the park . . .) and tell yourself that you can only do that thing after you've written some reasonable amount for the day. (Remember that the operative word here is "reasonable"; that is, what you can produce using some muscle, but not wearing yourself out.)

In my experience with dissertation writers, it's been rare for me to have to tell a writer that she's not writing enough. Far more often I'm in the paradoxical position of saying, "You're trying to write too much each day, and that's part of the reason you're stuck." Unreachable goals kill motivation. You need to evaluate realistically, not fantastically, what a reachable writing goal is for yourself, and then go for it. Each day that you succeed will make it easier for you to write the next day.

Go back and reread a few days' worth of writing from the last time you did manage to write anything in your dissertation, putting check marks next to interesting, or incomplete, passages. Then head up a new page with a line or two from one of these checked paragraphs and see if you can use it as a diving board back into your subject: "As I was writing two weeks ago, the really interesting question raised by X about this topic has several different possible answers. . . ." And then, if you're lucky, you're back in.

Look again at the notes you wrote while parking on the downhill slope, and see if you've fully elaborated each of them. That is, mine some of the smaller nuggets you've left strewn in earlier writing as a way of reminding yourself that you did at least once upon a time have some interesting things to say about your subject. You can use this strategy to give yourself the heart to move forward.

Return to freewriting with a vengeance. Try freewriting five pages a day, producing total junk if necessary, but preferably writing about anything in the world that causes you to have strong feelings. It is unlikely that your resistance can hold out for five full pages; it is likely that you will begin to write something.

Take the bull by the horns, and try writing about why you think you're stuck. Ask yourself questions, look for clues: how long have you been stuck, since when, what was going on then?

If you can unearth a reason ("It's the anniversary of my best friend's death, and I'm too depressed to write," "My advisor's comments on my last chapter left me feeling discouraged and angry," "I read that essay by Professor Z and began worrying that someone would scoop my ideas, so I got frightened"), you may find yourself able to write again. An inexplicable writing block is, for some of us, the scariest kind.

In "The Watcher at the Gates," Gail Godwin has some wonderful thoughts about how we get in our own way, and some funny solutions, among them these: "Write too fast for [your watcher] in an unexpected place, at an unexpected time. . . . Write when very tired. Write in purple ink on the back of a Master Charge statement."

Be a blatant behaviorist and bribe yourself shamelessly: "If I write today, I can call up my friend in Europe afterward and speak for five minutes," "If I write three pages today, tomorrow, and the next day, I can take most of that third day off, not read in the afternoon, and go to the beach instead."

Even more sensibly, try not to let yourself get stuck in the first place. Here are some good preventive strategies:

1. Create and care for your writing addiction. One of the most useful parts of such an addiction is that you'll get withdrawal symptoms if you don't write. If you've ever tried to break a serious addiction—smoking cigarettes, for example—you know that the threat of withdrawal symptoms is one of the most powerful deterrents to quitting. Here is one exception to the principle that negative reinforcement doesn't work well, and you can use this threat to keep yourself writing: "I will feel terrible if I don't write today."

2. Always park on the downhill slope. Writing on the downhill slope on Monday is a wonderfully simple way to jump-start your writing on Tuesday, because you've already done the hardest part of the job of beginning: you've decided what you're going to write about. (If you should change your mind partway through, it's easy; just write about your new topic and make sure you park on the downhill slope at the end of Tuesday.)

3. Write first.

4. Don't cry over spilt milk, or unwritten pages. The AA folks are onto something terribly important when they encourage each other to live "one day at a time." Change that motto to "write one day at a time," and then live by it. What does this mean in action? It means, don't waste your energy on worrying either about next week's writing or about yesterday's, either done or not done. If you want to be self-destructive, you can make the fact that you only wrote two lines yesterday have a great effect on today's writing—most likely to "make you" write only one line today. Negative reinforcement really doesn't work most of the time, unless your real goal is to make yourself feel lousy.

If you try to beat yourself into writing more today because you wrote less yesterday, you'll either end up not producing today, or producing a lot—and then you'll get so caught up in the guilt and repentance cycle that you'll produce nothing tomorrow, and so on. If we go back to the starting assumption that you really do want to write your dissertation, the best way to proceed is as if one day's production has absolutely nothing to do with any other day's. You *are* permitted, of course, to use the *positive* feelings generated by a successful day's, or week's, writing to encourage yourself—in fact, you should.

5. Remember one of the best rewards of all: the writing you hold in your hand. Except for those neurotic folks who can manage instantly not to be pleased by anything they write, the most powerful rewards for screwing up your courage and writing are the process itself, the feeling that your writing is once again on track, and the lovely shuffle of finished pages in your hand.

7

You, Your Readers, and
the Dissertation Support Group

Writing for Yourself and for Others

MOST OF THE GRADUATE students I meet while they're writing their theses are doing so for the best of all possible reasons, particularly in these years of a lean academic job market: they want to be able to commit their time to thinking about, researching, and writing up a project in which they have a deep interest. God knows, in struggling through a doctoral dissertation there are relatively few external rewards along the way, except for unregenerate masochists: the hours are endless, the pay is nonexistent, and the outside recognition extremely rare. Many of us who have lived through this process successfully have been driven by a powerful need to know and investigate something, and to write down the results of our investigation. We put together words in our search for truths, and it is the process in and of itself that rewards us for the time and energy it takes to produce a dissertation. In this way, we write for ourselves.

We also write for ourselves in another way: in the early stages of writing a dissertation your major audience is often yourself. That is, you write to explain your subject to yourself, and to make sense of it for yourself. Only after you've done that, if you're lucky, do you worry about how to present it to others, to your thesis advisor, committee members, fellow graduate students. When you reach that stage, you also reach a stage of revision that begins to include thinking about your external audience. This shift, when it comes at the right time, can produce a powerful difference in your writing, as you struggle to make yourself clear: to turn your private utterances into public ones, to overcome ellipses, to find an appropriate tone and make your language precise. But before this point, you are often alone in and with your work.

Writing seriously is a lonely process; loneliness is a frequent complaint of dissertation writers, even as they acknowledge that too much company distracts them. When you reach the stage in your thesis when it's time to first invite selected, and then more general, others to hear what you've said, you also reconnect to other people, to other thinkers who can help you, with their different ideas and styles, to expand your own thinking and writing.

First you write for yourself, toward the truths you are attempting to discover. Then you write for yourself, but with a gradually increasing objectivity about the piece—you listen for the word that sounds harsh, you think about what you've said and see a hole in your argument, you look at your plan for the whole project and realize that you've bitten off too large a topic—and you work to fix each of these things, incrementally. You begin to work, that is, at hearing yourself as you want later readers to hear you.

Next you begin to write explicitly to be heard by others, and here you do the convoluted mental gymnastics required to imagine someone else's mind meeting your writing: what will someone who is well acquainted with this material think of what you have written? Have you explained your new take on the topic sufficiently to convince her? How about a reader less acquainted with the specifics of your field? Will there be such readers of this paper? What will your advisor, who has a bee in her bonnet about one aspect of the work, think of an argument that disagrees with hers? Have you worked hard enough to convince her? Have you convinced yourself? As you work back and forth between the external and the internal audience, you are writing, finally, for both: writing to be heard by yourself and by others.

You and Your Readers

You have to be quite careful, though, which others you invite to read your early writing; many writers are quite vulnerable to any criticism at this stage. Several years ago Helen Benedict, a professor at Columbia University's Graduate School of Journalism, wrote a wonderful short essay called "A Writer's First Readers," in which she describes that vulnerability and talks about how professional writers deal with it. She quotes Cynthia Ozick's summary of the stakes: "If we had to say what writing is, we would have to define it essentially as an act of courage." Nancy Mairs, writing in *Voice Lessons*, tells us that this sensitivity doesn't go away: "If the very thought of taking off all your clothes in the middle of the Washington Mall during a school holiday makes you blush, you haven't even begun to dream what it feels like to publish a book." You need to think hard about whom you will trust with your early attempts; if you're fortunate, your advisor or one or more of your committee members might be such persons. Or a partner or close friend can fill this role. Fellow graduate students in the midst of the same initiation rite are sometimes useful, so long as you set up ground rules in advance to protect you all from the competition that's often endemic among classmates. There are no oughts here— but you should choose as an early reader someone who is most likely to help you get to the next stage; that means someone whom you can trust, with whom you feel comfortable.

Think very realistically about what you want from your reader. Your requirements are almost sure to change at various stages in your dissertation project. At the beginning, for example, you might want someone to cast his eyes over your chapter, but not say anything at all (unless he can't help a spontaneous exclamation of delight at the brilliance of your ideas). Writers who either haven't had a lot of experience with direct feedback or who don't realize just how powerful an effect it can have on their ability to work sometimes make a serious mistake in approaching their readers: they ask too early for "everything you think about this piece, all the mistakes you can find in it." Fortunately, many readers recognize both the dissertation writer's vulnerability and what early drafts look like, and they do not accept the writer's invitation to rip apart his first draft.

Then there are the readers from hell, who like to go for the jugular early on. You have to arm yourself properly against them, remembering that you own this piece of writing, and that you are entitled to ask for, and get, the kind of feedback that you think will be most useful to you, and most encouraging of your work. Cynthia Ozick describes the effect of a nasty rejection on her ability to write a novel: "I lost six months in despair before I could get back to it. I was nothing and nobody and working in the dark and old already, and the amount of destruction was volcanic." Even if the harsh reader is your advisor, you can probably still find a way to let her know that you need something else; oftentimes, if you're firm enough, you can get it. And if you can't, pick other readers to review your piece at this early stage in the way you feel you need it read. Use them as antidotes, and have them standing by to comfort you. In the very worst case, if you feel as though you won't be able to write at all in the face of your advisor's criticism, think seriously about finding a new advisor. But consider first fighting back and getting energy from the thought of proving her wrong.

A good advisor will respond to your changing needs as your project changes: in the beginning, she'll mostly offer encouragement and advice to keep writing. She will listen to you as you try to clarify your arguments, will point out inconsistencies or holes, and will ask you questions that will help you get at what it is you're really trying to say, what order your ideas might be presented in. She will offer criticisms that will help you move in useful directions, but she should not pick out every flaw in your early drafts. In later drafts she will stand in for the harder critics out there in the world: "How will you answer X, who believes that this theory of yours won't hold water? This argument doesn't do it." Pray that someone on your committee is really interested in writing and can point you toward editing the style of your dissertation so that not only your ideas but also your expression of them are elegant. Later on, your advisor's and committee members' job is to help you discover as many flaws as possible in your thesis, so that the document you ultimately put out in the world will represent you in a way that will make you proud.

You will also ask yourself to be flexible, and to grow up, as you write. In the beginning you'll allow yourself to be gentle with your dissertation, but later on, push yourself to be able to tolerate criticism, to keep your mind open, to not hold onto your words out of sheer stubbornness or arrogance or conservatism. Paradoxically, it's essential that you remember through all the stages of your work that you are the first and last owner of your words, that you get to make the ultimate editorial decisions. If you can learn to do this in the course of writing your dissertation, you will not only produce a fine dissertation; you will also learn both to think and to write.

The Dissertation Support Group

One of the best ways you can involve other people in your dissertation work is by forming a support group. Such a group can provide you with several important things: Properly chosen, it can offer you the good company of other people who are in the same boat as you, a terrific way of addressing the isolation that troubles so many dissertation writers. Having a group frees you from having to scramble again and again to make ad hoc arrangements with other people. The right group creates a supportive atmosphere—and a reliable, known bunch of people who know you and your work and can empathize, criticize, and push, as the occasion demands, *with the expectation that you will do the same for them*. It also provides additional structure in your dissertation-writing life: established, regular meeting times at which you know you have to show up, tell people what you've been doing, and give an accounting of what you have (and haven't) accomplished since you last met—these are the best sort of deadlines!

The thesis support group I belonged to in graduate school worked beautifully; I still have warm memories of it. There were six of us in the group, all from the same department, both men and women; some of us were friends, some just classmates. One of the most useful features of the group was that its members were at different stages in the thesis-writing process. I joined the year before I got my degree, when I had my data and some early writing done; another group member was at about the same place. Two others were at an earlier stage and hadn't yet begun writing; the last two were in the thick of their dissertations, sprinting toward that year's deadline. My first year in the group I proofread the dissertation of one of the front-runners; the following year, one of the members who was then in the midst of his thesis proofread mine. The sense of continuity and of the proper balance of giving and taking in that small writing community were deeply satisfying.

That support group illustrates some important choices you have to make in setting up your own. What's the composition of your group going to be: students from a single department or several? Are the members going to be at the same stage in the dissertation-writing process, or at different stages? Will they be all men, all women, or a mixture of both? Is the group going to be leaderless or led by some expert? What sort of help do you hope to offer each other?

Define what you want from your group. Here are some useful possibilities: good company at predictable times; a cheerleading squad; your first, trustworthy readers; the kind of company that misery loves; role models who are similar to you;

people to bounce ideas off or talk with about places in your work where you're stuck; people who give you an occasion to set meaningful deadlines; people who expect you to meet the deadline you've set; people who threaten public shaming if you blow off your deadline, but will offer sympathy and help if you've really tried to meet it but gotten stuck (or the flu). All of these benefits fall under the rubric of "good company." In a group with an experienced leader, or in a multistage group, you can also expect good advice on how you might proceed, and on what it is important to think about next.

Here are some things that you might also wish a group to do for you, but that aren't reasonable to expect: listen to you kvetch, week after week, about how you can't get any work done; read your mind about the sort of feedback you'd like; listen to your personal problems; think your work is more important than their own; write your dissertation for you, revise it for you, edit it for you (proofreading's fine, if you can get it, and if you're willing to reciprocate); convince you that the work you insist on calling garbage is great, whether or not it is; deal with your neuroses.

In setting up a dissertation support group, you need to consider the group parameters, one by one. For example, there are some powerful advantages to having a group made up entirely of grad students in your department: you will speak a common language and probably be struggling with similar kinds of issues. As a first professional audience for your ideas and writing, this kind of group can be great. If you're struggling with your advisor, the group members will know whom you're talking about, and they may be able to help. But there are also some real disadvantages to this setup. It can be politically delicate, should you feel the need to complain out loud about your advisor, to do this in the presence of other people in your department. More important, though, is the issue of competition: such a group can, at its worst, re-create the nastiest aspects of sibling rivalry, particularly if some of you share an advisor. Whether or not this happens depends in part on individual personalities, but it also depends in part on your advisor, and whether he is fair and equitable to advisees and doesn't, subtly or otherwise, play one off against another. I've seen, at the extremes, both sorts of advisor: my own thesis advisor's students often ended up as friends, a tribute to her generosity and dedication to collaborative work, but I've also heard stories about advisors increasing their own sense of power by pitting students against each other for the few favors the advisor was willing to dispense.

On the issue of trust: You may be feeling hesitant to talk in a group situation about the new ideas you've discovered, because of the risk, real, or imagined, that your ideas will end up in someone else's work. Dissertation writers are notoriously paranoid, but this doesn't mean that ideas never get misappropriated or, more bluntly, stolen. What to do about this? Be careful, particularly in choosing your group members. Think about discussing the issues of ownership, trust, and scrupulousness at the very beginning of the group's meetings. Stick with small groups. Protect any material that feels vulnerable to others' conscious, or unintentional, appropriation. If you think you have good cause to be nervous about the trustworthiness of someone in the group, make sure you collect up all the copies of your work at the end of each meeting. And consider a heterogeneous field group, where such concerns are less likely to be an issue.

An interdepartmental group is likely to focus more on writing and on questions about the process of producing the dissertation than on the specifics of subject matter, since most of the members are likely to be unacquainted with the particular content of a field different from their own. This is not necessarily a disadvantage. Having your work read by a smart person outside your field can be a terrific way to find out if your writing makes sense, and if your argument flows well: someone already acquainted with your material is more likely to fill in any gaps from her own knowledge.

There is no single right way to set up a support group, just advantages and disadvantages to each choice. So, for example, having friends in the group can help you feel more comfortable, but it can also make the interpersonal dynamics more complicated. Having everyone at the same stage, say, just beginning to think about writing, can create solidarity: "We're all in the same boat." But it can also foster destructive, as well as useful, competition, or mutual panic. The single-stage group has one more inherent problem: all of you are probably equally ignorant of what the next stage looks like.

As for single-sex versus mixed groups, there are some fields in which it's more likely that you'll end up with a single-sex discussion group (women's studies comes to mind). I've met with many dissertation support groups that are set up as single-sex groups, and I have seen both their advantages and their disadvantages. Sometimes there's a greater comfort level in single-sex groups, where men or women feel freer to speak in gendered language and are liberated from the kind of posturing that people sometimes engage in (consciously or otherwise) in the presence of the opposite sex. Women often complain that they feel silenced by men in groups, and men sometimes believe that women spend too much time on touchy-feely issues or that women are too vulnerable to criticism. Granted, each of these complaints may be either stereotyped or stereotypical behavior, but you probably don't want to have to fight the gender wars while you're worrying about your dissertation.

Remember, the professional world you will enter after graduate school is unlikely to be single sex. And single-sex groups have their problems too: more competition—unpleasant in different ways in men's versus women's groups, but unpleasant nevertheless—and usually characterized by less variety of thought and criticism. When a mixed group works well, with different styles of readers and writers contributing their strengths and their differences to the group, and diluting the intense games that are sometimes more easily played in single-sex groups, they are probably the most interesting and productive sort—individual personalities permitting, of course!

The last of the issues you have to consider before you go about creating your support group is whether you are going to have a leaderless group, a group in which the members rotate the leadership among themselves, or a more formal leader, most likely a faculty member or perhaps someone who specializes in consulting to dissertation writers. In *Writing Without Teachers*, Peter Elbow has laid out, probably for all time, the territory of the leaderless writing group, describing its process as well as strategies for setting it up so it works. He suggests seven to twelve group members and a meeting at least once a week in which everyone reads and responds to everyone else's writing. Elbow recommends that the group meet for at least a few months and that each person write something to bring to the meeting every week. (His section on the details of responding to other people's work is particularly strong, and too long to excerpt here.) Be forewarned, though, that such a group requires a very high level of commitment from each of its members, and that such a group can, at its worst, feel like being in a country in which the blind lead the blind. When leaderless groups work well, though, they are the easiest and least formal way to go about getting the support you need.

Despite their possible advantages—greater comfort because there's no need to put on a face for the teacher, and a sense of equality—leaderless groups also face some possible hazards: no one minding the store; no guidance from someone who knows about the whole process of creating a dissertation, who can offer help when needed; no strong hand to intervene if and when the group gets off course. To counter this, you can take turns being group leader, to keep order and encourage forward momentum; share among you the work of searching for resources and advice that you then bring back to the group; and include group members who are at different stages in the dissertation process.

It can also work well to have a dissertation support "group" with just one other person, particularly if you already know that you can work well with that person. If you are writing at a distance from the university where you've studied, working with one other person might be an especially useful choice (you can also check out larger groups if you're resident in another university community).

Having decided on the kind of group you want, how do you go about setting it up? Where do you find the group members? How do you find a group leader if you want one? How do you set up the parameters of the group so it will work well? First check whether such groups already exist at your university. I've known of dissertation advisors who have set up and led groups for their own students (a particularly useful mode for the kind of popular thesis advisor who has so many thesis students that she can't meet as frequently as she'd like to with each of them alone). Some university departments run dissertation support groups for their students, and universities that have writing centers or academic support centers sometimes sponsor groups through those offices (or they might consider doing so if you suggest it). Graduate student organizations, either within a department or universitywide, are another possible source. You might also ask your advisor, contact the graduate studies office or your department or dean for help with how you might connect with other students who are looking for the same sort of company.

But you might already know of potential members. Ask your peers if they're interested; ask around at department coffee hours or events. If this doesn't work, design an attractive ad and put it up in places where people like you might read the bulletin board. If your department is lucky enough to have an administrator who runs everything and knows everyone, ask him if he knows of others who are looking for a group, or ask him to put the word out that you are. Or you might try a message on the in-house E-mail, or an ad in the university newspaper if it's the sort of publication you yourself would read. If you're not in residence at the place where you're earning your degree, you're going to have to work harder to provide yourself with decent writing company. But in either case, you don't, after all, need dozens of people—a few will do.

So once you've got the people, how do you structure the group? First you might consider a leaderless group; to see if it sounds stylistically compatible with the way you all like to work, discuss some of the issues you might have to deal with, and remind yourselves of strategies that will be helpful no matter what sort of group you choose. Then you think (and write and talk) seriously together about what your goals are for the group—what does each of you wish for and expect to get from the group?—because such expectations will help determine the answers to questions such as how often you will meet, for how long each time, how you set the agenda, and what that agenda will be. Make your goals specific and realizable; we all, particularly dissertation writers, have fantasies of perfect, always-available readers and editors, but remember that those are fantasies. The frequency and duration of your meetings can range from a few times a year for a couple of hours to once a week for a year. I think more is better. Much better, in fact.

Setting Up a Dissertation Support Group: A Checklist

____ Have you reached a point in your writing where you feel ready to talk with other students about your work? (Not necessarily comfortable, just ready.)

____ Do you know what you expect from such a group? Are your expectations realistic, and have you enjoyed, but discarded, your fantasy expectations?

____ Are you looking for a group composed of students who are all in your department, or one that includes people from various departments?

____ How frequently do you want to meet with such a group?

____ How big a group do you want? Just one other person or a larger group?

____ Do you prefer a single-sex or a mixed group?

____ Should the group be leaderless or led?

____ Have you decided where you'll look for such a group and made a list of the possibilities to check out (for example, talking with your advisor, the department administrator, the graduate student office, student support services, or other students and/or sending out an E-mail announcement or putting up an ad)?

The Dissertation Support Group: Expectations, Problems, and Negotiations

What's left to consider? You—both you the individual, and the collective you of the group—should plan to spend the first meeting or two agreeing on the parameters of the group. You'll have some negotiations about calendars, timing, and expectations. Try to make as much as you can think of explicit, for example, "So we've agreed that each of us will bring a one-page description of our project—with copies for all—to the next meeting and be prepared to spend ten minutes talking about our work plan and goals," or "We'll take turns bringing the snacks," or "We'll make a very serious effort to start on time, confining all chatting to before or after our meetings." By the end of the second meeting of the group it's reasonable to expect that the rules will be in place, and that you will have some sense of other people's work, and they of yours, each of you having already put a small sample of your writing out on the table for the group to see.

Farther along you may run into knots: someone regularly comes late or monopolizes the group's energy; people who promise to bring their writing fail to; feedback on writing is too harsh or too undiscriminating or just not helpful. Which brings me to the thesis group member from hell (GMFH). Anyone who's been a group leader has met this person, who exists in a variety of forms. The one constant is that he is capable, single-handedly, of destroying a group, and this holds true for informal thesis or book groups as well as for therapy groups. Here are some possible incarnations of the GMFH: the person who is so needy that his agenda takes up most of the group's time and energy; the person who, as a reader/critic, behaves like an unreliable attack dog; the person who is so fragile that serious criticism of his work feels impossible and cruel; the person who is so competitive that everyone else feels like hiding their manuscripts; the motormouth who wastes the group's time. A leaderless group is more vulnerable to the destructiveness of any of these difficult characters; a group with an effective leader can expect that the leader will make such a person either shape up or leave. Some group members from hell have serious personality disorders; others have bad habits that they are oblivious to—the latter can be reformed, with some constructive criticism. The best thing to do about a potential GMFH is to try to screen him out in advance: if you already know that one of your fellow students is needy and difficult well beyond the norm for your basic neurotic grad student, do not give in to your charitable impulses to help out by including this character in your thesis group. Instead you might encourage him to make weekly appointments with his thesis advisor. You will all get more work done this way.

Whichever problem the group encounters, it's important to remember that this is a *work* group, not a tea party, and to take up whatever problem arises quickly, straightforwardly, and calmly as something to be negotiated and solved. *Not* doing so will prove to be much more painful than suffering through the short-lived awkwardness that comes with tending to the group's business. If you find yourself really stuck, call in a consultant—

an outsider, such as a dissertation advisor or someone from the university study center, who can help you identify and solve the problem.

· · ·

A thesis support group that works well can offer you important gifts: a cheering squad, readers, trustworthy critics and editors, people who encourage you to set goals, hold you to them, and keep you good company at the various stages of what is otherwise, for most of us, most of the time, a solitary journey.

8

Revising: The Second Draft and Beyond

ONE OF THE BEST-KEPT writing secrets around is that the more you revise, the clearer, more fluid, and more natural your writing will be. It's not inspiration but hard work that produces simple, elegant writing. In chapter 4 I've written about the process that takes you from a mess to a first draft. In this chapter I'll consider the shift from your first (or early draft) to a finished product. By this time in your academic career you either know, or you can invent, specific strategies for reworking your prose; in the following pages I'll focus primarily on the psychology of revision.

Thinking About the Revision Process

I didn't really learn how to revise my own writing until I was working on my doctoral dissertation. I had been, before then, a facile enough writer so that I could do a little bit of cutting and pasting, and some proofreading, and hand in a finished enough paper. Some of you have probably gotten away with doing glorified proofreading and calling it "revision." Having to revise

116

their dissertation in major ways makes some writers feel as if they've done something wrong with their first draft—that if they had done it right the first time, it wouldn't require massive rethinking at this later stage. In fact, if you're facing major revisions of your dissertation, you've probably done something right.

When I was a young writer, I had very little interest in revision. The idea of hacking at words I'd already managed to get down on paper, to change or even to discard them, struck me as both unpleasant and dangerous. I didn't fundamentally believe that I could make anything better by working at it. Partly I didn't believe it because I didn't realize that, like any job worth doing, writing takes stamina. I didn't know it was possible to get tired of a piece of writing, or bored with it, and come back to it anyway. But behind these feelings of boredom or exhaustion were more frightening ones: I didn't really believe that I had any more words where those first ones had come from, so tampering with or discarding any of the ones I had already set down felt risky. I wanted to leave them be, to think I was finished with them when I wasn't, not to raise doubts or the spectre that I might, if I looked too closely, discover I had said nothing and had nothing to say.

Because I was able to write quick, nearly finished first drafts, I had never found out how good a writer I might be. Revising my writing would mean exploring my limits, perhaps deciding to push them; but I would probably also have to give up my fantasy that by working hard enough, I could write like Virginia Woolf. The other terror, of making myself clear, was even greater. I responded by writing in a private language. When readers said they couldn't understand what I was talking about, I was both distressed and secretly relieved. As I grew older I found

I had some things I wanted to say and have heard. At that point it became necessary for me to speak in the common tongue, and to revise.

To make your writing really clear is also to make yourself very vulnerable. If someone can find out from your writing what you believe, or how you feel, or where you stand, then you may be liked or disliked, agreed or disagreed with, congratulated or criticized for what you've written. As long as you stay hidden in opaque or obscure writing, you're safe. Don Graves puts this dilemma succinctly: "You have to be willing to be a professional nudist if you're going to write." If you are having some trouble making yourself clear in writing, consider whether you really want to.

What is your usual revision practice? Do you revise the life out of a piece, or do you get so caught up in the details that you forget your train of thought? Or do you not revise enough, because you are afraid to look too closely at your writing lest you discover a fatal flaw? We all want to get all of it right the first time. But in writing, as with most skills worth developing, you have to know how to undo the mistakes you will inevitably make (knitting projects come to mind) before you can become accomplished. Revision is a way to think further about your subject, to say something in the clearest possible way, and to undo mistakes, all in the service of producing first-rate writing.

Here's another way to think about revision: When you revise, imagine yourself as a reader, instead of the writer, and ask yourself, "Does this make sense to me?" But you are a very privileged reader, because if you don't like what you see or hear *you can change it.* Some writers actually enjoy revising more than they do creating the original draft, because the pressure to generate material is off. When revising, what you're engaged in is closer to craft than it is to art, and if you keep at it long enough, you'll succeed without having to worry about inspiration.

Observe your own style carefully: Do you tend to pour out early draft stuff and then spend most of your time cleaning up the mess? Or, when you read your first draft, do you see that you don't have enough material, that you need to generate more? Perhaps most important to remember is that revision is about staying open—to change and to new ideas and new ways of expressing them. If you can manage this frame of mind, you'll not only produce a richer piece of work; you'll also keep yourself much more interested in your project. Once you commit yourself to being open to change, you'll begin to figure out how to make the changes you need to make.

Dissertations can be organizational nightmares, even if you begin with a complete and careful outline of the whole. If you are allowing your material to grow and change, it is very likely to outgrow your careful outline. You will have unexpected ideas, and the ones you already have will become more elaborate, or they may prove to be inaccurate; you'll see connections or contradictions you didn't notice before. You'll find yourself moving misplaced sentences and paragraphs around, combining some chapters and axing others. You'll notice that the terrific argument you were saving for chapter 4 really needs to be in chapter 2, because it has to precede what's in chapter 3.

One of the hardest parts of a dissertation project is that there is so much of it to keep track of and think about, all at the same time. Such a project is just too big to hold it all in your head at once, and too complex to get it right the first time. In the past, writing course papers, even some as long as forty or fifty pages, maybe it was possible for you to imagine the shape of the whole; you were probably making a single argument, no matter how elaborate it was. But the structure of your dissertation is very different from that of even a very long paper. Now you are putting together several chapters, each of them the length of those course papers. Revision issues that came up in individual essays are writ large in your dissertation: transitions from one chapter to another are more complicated than those from one paragraph to the next; repetitions are harder to catch when a point comes up in different chapters; consistency—of voice, vocabulary, angle of approach—is harder to sustain over many pages, some of them written months apart. Because of all of these differences you can't usually write a decent dissertation without doing at least as much work revising as you did composing your original draft. So even if you've never revised, you're going to have to begin now.

Useful Revision Strategies

Although I've promised to concentrate mostly on the psychology of revision, there are some strategies it's useful for you to know. Here's a checklist that will help you approach the task:

___ Work on one chapter at a time until you're well along in the process; only then should you struggle with the final shape of the whole, since that will shift many times in the course of your writing.
___ Consider leaving the revision of both the introduction and the conclusion until last.
___ When you're unsure of your argument or the shape of a

chapter, try making an outline of what you have. Problems show up much more clearly in outline form, as well as in the process of making the outline.

___ Use the outline on a smaller scale: try reducing each paragraph of a chapter to one sentence. When you can't do it, you'll discover which paragraphs are incomplete or fuzzy. By writing one sentence to cover each paragraph you'll be able, by looking at the sentences you've created, to scrutinize the flow of your argument.

___ Leave editing at the individual word level for last, unless the word that concerns you is one that's crucial to your argument.

___ Similarly, leave smoothing the transitions from paragraph to paragraph for a late stage, because paragraphs will come and go, and they will move around as you work your argument. There's no point in making an elegant transition you won't be able to use.

___ Remember the saddest rule of editing: less is more. Delete any word that isn't necessary (particularly adjectives), and you'll strengthen your point.

___ Use your ears. Read your prose aloud, to catch awkward turns of phrase and redundancies. How does it sound? This is a good method for finding the sentences that tie themselves in knots.

___ Have someone else read your work and look for phrases that you've unconsciously overused or arguments you've repeated. It's hard to notice such things when you've written them.

___ Use your eyes. It matters to your reader how your page looks: a page that's all one paragraph is daunting to read; one that consists of very short paragraphs looks superficial.

___ Use your breath. If you can't read a sentence aloud without turning blue, it either needs more punctuation or should be cut into more than one sentence.

___ Watch out for your writing quirks, such as overusing particular words or punctuation (I'm rather fond of dashes, myself). And vary your sentences—many of us are prone to overusing sentences of a particular shape or length, and this makes for boring reading.

___ Keep a thesaurus, a dictionary, and a style manual at hand when you're revising. Check out which style manual is standard in your own field, but for reference, *The Chicago Manual of Style* is superb and complete. The thesaurus is both useful and fun—and indispensable for varying your word choice (how many ways can you say "dissertation" or "writing"?).

___ Remember—hard as this is to do when you're wading through the mess—that you can afford to cut words because there are more where those came from.

___ Don't use complex language or jargon when simple words will make your point equally well. Rather than using putting-on-airs language, go for elegant simplicity.

___ When you think you're done with editing, read the chapter again. And then again. It's amazing how many times you can go round and still catch errors or infelicities you'd be embarrassed to discover in the finished work.

___ Remember that Ernest Hemingway rewrote the last sentence of *A Farewell to Arms* thirty-nine times.

___ And, paradoxically, realize you'll never get your dissertation perfect, that at some point you'll have to quit fiddling with it and send it off into the world.

There is no magical method: revising means rethinking and rewriting, again and again and again, until you feel like you've gotten it right. Some people can do this solo, by casting a cold, steely gaze on their own writing. Others are more timid and need to involve kindhearted readers who can say, gently but firmly, things like, "I can't understand what you're trying to say here," or "I liked this, but I thought it contradicted the idea you discussed on page 2." Some people work best revising by categories: first for overall organization, then for clarity of thought, and so on; I can only do it by looking at everything at once, seeing what stands out for me as I reread again and again. No matter which method you use, each time you read through, write yourself lots of notes, either in the margin of your draft or on a pad of paper, keying your comments to particular paragraphs or pages. This way you won't lose track of your different readings: the sense that you have on the first reading that you don't understand a sentence, or on the second that there's something wrong with a transition, or on the third that the writing really seems O.K.

It can also be very useful to make the transition from creation to revision explicit, by marking it with rituals: you might, for example, do your revising in a different place than you do your first draft. You might change not only the place, but also the mode: compose in pen and ink and revise on the computer, or vice versa.

Your zero draft can be described as the pure outpouring of prose that just comes. Revision involves making important rational choices: of what stance to take, of speaking voice, of words and sounds, of kinds of argument, and of what is to be included or excluded. As you reread your draft, you will make such choices at different levels, from the overall shape of your argument to where the commas go. In the earliest drafts of your chapters you probably wrote as if talking to yourself—how you felt about your subject; your own slant on it; your questions, concerns, and irritation with it; your attempts to wrestle it to the ground. At the revision stage of your thesis you will write much more explicitly for your audience.

Revision requires stamina: you can't quit just because you're tired, or because you don't ever want to see one particular paragraph again, or because you hope the writing is O.K., even though you know it isn't. You can take a break, or alternate revising with other kinds of work: looking up references or working on other short projects, so that you don't have to do it all at once. But the biggest temptation for most people (leaving aside the obsessives, who can't *stop* revising) is to quit too soon. We're all prone to wishful thinking, hoping that someone else will magically understand what we mean, even though we haven't said it very well, or that our writing will somehow have improved between the time we put it down and when we pick it up again. If you keep revising even though you feel unenergetic and bored, you may, if you're lucky, find yourself becoming more interested as you proceed. It helps to set yourself a goal for each revision session ("I will work my way all the way through this section before I quit for lunch," or "I'm going to check out every transition in these next ten pages," or "I'm going to read through and see if I think I could understand this stuff if I didn't already know it"). Just as it's O.K. to be scared, it's also O.K. to be tired or bored, just so long as you keep working anyway.

Revision and Truth Telling

Questions of truth telling are central to the dissertation. This quest begins with the thesis proposal (which I often characterize as an exercise in lying, in pretending to know that which you cannot yet possibly know) and continues throughout the writing of the dissertation. (For example, how candid are you going to be about your presuppositions? About the research glitches along the way? About how firmly you believe your results? About how happy you are with them? About what you've chosen to put into, or leave out of, your argument? Which evidence you've suppressed, and which you've chosen to highlight?) As soon as you begin to act on your data, of whatever sort, you are dealing with questions of truth, with the trade-offs between pure "story" and the artful creation of the "plot" that make for a coherent narrative. Even in a dissertation that is a musical composition, the composer makes certain compromises with pure inspiration to increase the chances that her creation will be performed.

As you revise the original, early draft of your work, you may find that as you shape, fashion, cut, add, and work your early words, what you end up with begins to feel more like artifice and less like truth, because your writing is less natural. Certainly your later version of your text is not as spontaneous as the first version. But even as it becomes "less true" in some ways, it is becoming more true in others. Another sad fact of revision is that as you prepare your writing for viewing by an audience other than yourself, you have to give up some parts of it— perhaps the private joke, perhaps the scurrilous remark about the critic you dislike, perhaps the language that is too strong for others' eyes. This is the time to acknowledge that you can't always say everything you want to say, because what you might want to say could conflict with the politics of being a graduate student or a job applicant, or it could simply make your dissertation less readable, or less read, by your intended audience.

You need to decide at this point what part of your argument *really* holds water, and what part of it is the product of your wishful thinking ("Wouldn't it be lovely if these data really proved that Shakespeare was a woman?"). Those decisions will affect the truth of your text. You will have to struggle with understanding your own work, and with giving up the hope that others can read your mind. You will come to see that writing and revision are gradual processes by which you make yourself clearer both to your audience and to yourself.

Revision is a search for closer and closer approximations of the truth you seek; but even though you halve the inaccuracies of your text with each iteration, you will never reach the perfect text you're striving for, because it exists only in fantasy. What matters is that you work your way *toward* that text, toward the truest narrative that you can achieve, one that speaks clearly and fluently to your chosen audience.

9

The Best Dissertation
Is a Done Dissertation

The Costs of Growth

IF YOU WERE a reader as a child, you may remember some books that you were very sad to finish. (*Peter Pan* and *The Secret Garden* were such books for me.) It's rare as an adult to get the chance to live for a while in a fully fashioned, deeply textured fictional world. But there's a similar phenomenon that you can experience by writing your dissertation: for a privileged bit of time you can live in a world of your own choosing and making, a world that you've created in your mind, but one that you also have to leave behind.

William G. Perry Jr., who has worked with generations of students, once wrote a paper called "Sharing in the Costs of Growth." Its central question is this: How do we deal with the fact that there is sadness as well as joy about each major step we take forward—including finishing a doctoral degree? You may expect that you will feel only relief and pleasure when you earn your degree, so you may be startled by feelings of loss and sadness. Maybe you will grieve that a major stage of your life is over, or perhaps you will mourn the important people who are not alive to witness your triumph, or maybe you'll confront the gap between the dissertation you've actually written and the one you imagined you would write. For the last of these concerns there is consolation: the writing of a dissertation is usually only the first of many pieces of writing you'll produce in your life, and it's pretty rare for a thesis to win the Pulitzer; but the book a few years down the road, that had its original inspiration in those ideas of your thesis, might still . . .

Perry is right about the costs of growth, and his observation also applies to the feelings you may have about making progress on your dissertation. You may be surprised to find that you're not unambivalently delighted that you're progressing. I very rarely ask my clients what being about to complete a dissertation means to them, because I know how deep and charged the answer to that question often is. But even if the meaning is almost totally positive (with no tinges of "my boyfriend will hate me for being smarter than he is," or "my parents always wanted me to be a farmer," or "what sort of a woman has a Ph.D.?"), it's still hard to move on. Every major life change destroys the equilibrium of our lives and our self-image and leaves behind a portion of an old self. Most of us are on some level conservatives; even if the new self is better, we feel some sadness at leaving the old one. This sort of ambivalence is probably familiar to you: You may already have noticed that you don't feel all one way about your writing, that you may be capable of judging a particular piece of writing to be "garbage" one day and "terrific" the next. Ambivalent feelings are part of most of the things we do in life, particularly the important ones.

I've known several people who were the first ones in their families to earn a doctorate (as I was myself). Some of them were also the first to graduate from college. This particular scenario is a powerful example of the loyalty issues that can emerge in finishing a doctorate. Those of us who have been in this position experience a potent mixture of feelings, as do our families: pride, insecurity, dis/loyalty, misunderstanding, jealousy. We wonder if getting a doctorate will lose us our parents' love, or so separate us that there will never be any going home again; we worry that we've traded our place in the world we knew growing up for a foreign and insecure world, where no one "knew us when." These costs of growth are writ large in some of our psyches, and they may slow us down in our progress or sadden us even more than they sadden others who are not changing worlds along with changing academic status.

Hitting the Wall

If you've ever run a marathon, or watched one at about mile twenty, you'll know about this phenomenon: most of the way through the race many runners "hit the wall"; that is, suddenly they feel that they can go no farther, that they've exhausted not only their second wind but all subsequent ones. It's a paradoxical feeling, because in both mile twenty of a marathon and the equivalent stage of writing a dissertation you've already done most of the work. There's another kind of hitting the wall that sometimes happens to thesis writers: you feel an impossible barrier between you and the finish line, the bottom falls out of your hopefulness and ambition, and your spirits border on despair and collapse. I've more than once heard someone with less than five percent of her thesis left to write say, "I've decided not to go on with this project." This is a time when the demons can catch up with you, when every one of the internal creatures who got in your way all along decides to gang up on you just this side of the finish, to remind you of all the good reasons why you shouldn't finish your degree.

Getting On with It

Back in chapter 5 I warned you to keep a sustainable pace. But now, as you move into the final stages, you can afford to get wired, to overwork, to push yourself harder than ever before. You'll be amazed at how much work it's possible to accomplish in a month or two, if it's the *last* month or two. Samuel Johnson noted that "when a man knows he is to be hanged in a fortnight, it concentrates his mind wonderfully." Your work now is to keep up a steady, perhaps even accelerating pace, and to get yourself over the last hurdles—psychological, intellectual, or organizational. You also need to force yourself to revise your thesis up to a standard you'll be proud of, even though you may feel like just printing out whatever you've got and handing it in as is.

At this stage you'll need to deal with a lot of nuisance tasks: editing, formatting, completing the bibliography and footnotes. You'll also have to extricate from their grantors the last of any copyright permissions, a job that can take a disproportionate amount of time, so it's a good idea not to put it off to the last moment. Don't waste your own energy on these kinds of things. It is neither necessary nor required that you, personally, track down each of your footnotes—you can get help from a willing partner, or maybe an undergraduate looking for a part-time job or a fellow grad student who will work for you now if you promise to work for her later. Nor is it necessary for you to learn the complexities of your software at the eleventh hour, if there's someone else around who will do it for love or for money (if you anticipated this need and learned the software on an earlier, smaller project, you'll be much more relaxed now). If you are taking care of some of this work yourself, make sure you use every available laborsaving device—tech support lines (if your software was acquired legally), library reference desks available by phone, resources on the Internet—to make the work easier; even if your thesis has been more pleasure than pain, you've probably already suffered enough. When you move on to the last revisions, make sure to ask other people to proofread; you will be too familiar with your text to catch all the typos. Polish as much as you can stand to; in the event that you decide to turn your thesis into a book, you'll have less to do later.

One of the best sources of advice for dealing with last-minute jobs such as those just mentioned—or for using software to paginate or to integrate software and texts, or for answering questions about what quality paper you must print on and what sort of scrutiny the watermark is going to get from the graduate office secretary, and how long it will take the bindery to produce your book—is a grad student who has just gone through handing in her dissertation. Buy her coffee, or a drink, but get her to download in your direction the file in her head that contains such important details, before she forgets them all.

A Possible Horrible Scenario

What if you're very close to your deadline, and one day you receive a letter from the dean, informing you that your absolute deadline is a month or two closer than you were counting on—in fact, it's next week? (One of my favorite sayings is "Dates in calendar may be closer than they appear.") What now?

After you've picked yourself up off the floor, there are a few things you can do: first, you can avoid this horrible scenario by checking out *all* such deadlines in advance, preferably by asking a live person as well as reading carefully all the written rules. Most of the students I've worked with who have found themselves in this spot have reacted by going into solitary confinement and becoming phobic about using the telephone, but it makes much more sense to call people: your close friends, your advisor, and the graduate school. Having invested this much in your education, it is a rare graduate school that will kick you out at this point if you can present them with a plan and some indication that you have been making real progress toward finishing, even if a bit belatedly. Among my large acquaintance of grad students, I haven't known a single student who was refused an extension—so what if it was sometimes grudging? I've met far more administrators who worked to help such students finish than ones who got in the students' way.

The Thesis Defense

You need to investigate what you can expect at the thesis defense. Ask your advisor, people in the graduate school office, and other students in your own department who have been through the process. Is it a mere formality? How often does someone actually flunk a defense? How rough a time have other people been given by their committees? This sort of information will help you prepare. You might even negotiate with the members of your committee what you will be responsible for at the defense. I've known some students who have agreed in advance with their committee members on both the possible content and the range of questions that could be on their exams, as an aid to their studying. The more you can demystify the process before you walk into your exam, the better off you'll be. Try to go to someone else's defense before your own; defenders are often allowed to invite a few guests. Do a practice defense, making up a list of questions you suspect you'll be asked (make them hard), and have your friends act as examiners.

It used to be that one's fate was decided at the thesis defense, and you didn't know when you went in whether you were going to come out with a doctorate. Nowadays, though, by the time you get to your defense, the assumption is that you will pass it and finish your degree. Most graduate programs are much more careful than they used to be about monitoring the progress of their students and screening out early those whom they don't think will be able to make it. There are, in fact, at least three different defenses for most graduate students: negotiating the thesis proposal, the judgments your advisor makes of the real draft you hand in, and the official "defense." At each of these points you invite a good hard look at your work, check out that it's reasonable for you to proceed, and get advice about how best to do so.

How you approach your thesis defense can determine both how well you do at it and what you get out of it. You need to cultivate a consumer mentality: remember how much you've paid to get to this moment, and take advantage of the all-star cast (a.k.a. your committee members) you've assembled by asking *them* questions. Remember that this is the last time you're likely to be a student, and that you're right at the edge of becoming a colleague; act like a professional and an expert in your field, as part of proving to your committee that you are ready to make the shift. Prepare in advance by asking yourself the kinds of hard questions you think they might pose, and even, perhaps, figure out how you're going to explain your magnum opus to the member of your committee who is less conversant with your specific field (or to the committee member who hasn't read the dissertation before the defense). Ask if it's permissible to invite some supportive friends and relatives to come, to cheer you on (or to wait outside the door to catch you as you emerge).

If you can finish writing your dissertation, and what you've written doesn't come as a complete surprise to your advisor, because she's been reading drafts of your chapters all along, it is extremely unlikely that you will fail your defense. Your committee may well ask you to make revisions—expect that they will, and count yourself unusually blessed if the thesis is accepted as submitted. Even knowing this, the defense will still feel like a major test; this is as much because of what it stands for—the end of one major stage of your life, and moving on to the next—as because of what it actually is.

Remember the old joke about what one calls the person who graduates last in his medical school class: "doctor." The same holds true for those who just squeak by their thesis defenses. The best dissertation is an accepted dissertation. And no one will ever ask you about your performance at the event at which it was accepted.

By this final stage you will have had a lot of experience deciding which of your advisor's suggestions to take and which to turn down. This experience turns out to have some startling ramifications: when you defend your thesis it will become much clearer to you that you own this work, that such ultimate decisions are yours, and, what's more, that you most likely know more about your subject than anyone else does, including your advisor and your committee members. This realization is an important *private* graduation, a psychological parallel to the public ceremony.

Afterward

Your dissertation has been accepted, and you find yourself beginning to answer when people address you as "Doctor." What do you do with yourself now, freed from the albatross you lived with for many months or years? Rejoice. Despite the ambivalence you may feel, despite the debts (financial and/or personal) you may have incurred, despite your exhaustion, this is a time to celebrate the end of an important stage of your professional life. And to be proud of yourself. No one ever gets a doctorate as a gift, or a door prize. You've earned it.

And graduation? Virginia Woolf has awful things to say about academic regalia and commencement processions; she may have had good reason, but I still think they're both splendid. Rent the appropriate plumage and invite everyone you love, everyone who really cares about you, everyone who's following in your footsteps to come watch you march and witness your induction into a very old company of highly educated women and men. And then have a wonderful meal or a party. (If you're superstitious, ask a good friend to plan it.) In the next chapter I'll talk about life after the dissertation, but for now, enjoy your well-earned vacation, and allow yourself to take pleasure in a major accomplishment.

10

~

Life After
the Dissertation

I REMEMBER CLEARLY a day soon after I'd gotten my degree, when one of my kids answered the phone, and someone asked for "Doctor Bolker." My husband had had his Ph.D. for ten years. Without missing a beat, my offspring asked, "Which one?" Life after the dissertation is about changes—shifts in your status, in your identity, in the shape of your life and your work, and in the dissertation itself—and there is no going back.

Your new degree will make a difference both in the way others see you, and in the way you see yourself. In the course of your graduate training and dissertation writing you will change from a student who is seeking others' instruction and judgments to an expert in the field, an authority on your subject, someone who can be called upon to make judgments. You may find yourself invited to review for professional journals, asked for reprints of articles that originate in your dissertation, or consulted by struggling graduate students. You have become someone who has written the equivalent of a book, someone who has potentially changed, as Ray Huey has noted, "from being someone who reads to someone who is read."

Your advisor or members of your committee may treat you differently, more like a colleague and a peer, and less like a student. You now know about yourself (most of the time) that you can focus on and sustain effort toward a difficult goal, overcome obstacles, keep going even when you don't feel like it, and allow yourself to get something that you want.

Publishing Your Dissertation

Having finished your dissertation, you'll need to decide what you're going to do with it: leave it to gradually gather dust on your bookshelf, turn the chapters into journal articles, turn it into a book, or bury it in the backyard. There are good reasons both for publishing and for not publishing.

Reasons for Publishing

• Your topic captivates you, and you're not done with it. You'd like to polish this piece of work further.

• You've done an elegant piece of work, and you want to put it out in the world.

• You want to have a larger audience for your ideas and a broader dialogue with your readers.

• You're hoping to get an academic position, and publishing your dissertation will help you do so.

• You're hoping to have a "crossover" book: to turn your academic manuscript into a best-selling trade book.

• You've turned into a writer.

Reasons for Not Publishing

• You hate your dissertation. You honestly don't believe it's good (not just on alternate days).

- Your dissertation was on a topic of your advisor's choosing; now you've chosen your own subject and left the thesis subject behind.
- You've outgrown and are bored by your dissertation.
- You don't want to be an academic, or you're shifting fields.

There's always the chance that any of these reasons could be a rationalization, that what you really mean is, you're trying to gather together the energy to take a good hard look at your dissertation, to see if you want to reengage with it in an ongoing way. If you've written a good thesis (you'll know it, others will tell you so, your committee will be enthusiastic about it, or, in the absolutely best case, a publisher will approach you), don't put it aside permanently until you've allowed a bit of time to elapse and have tried approaching it again.

Publishing a Book or Separate Articles?

If you choose to publish your dissertation, how do you decide whether to transform it into articles or a book? What are the issues?

- Are you prepared to do the amount of work that turning your thesis into a book will entail?
- How important do you think your dissertation is in your field?
- Once you strip away the literature review, research design, and so forth, do you have a book's worth of new material? (The answer to this question in the sciences is almost always no. I've never heard of a science dissertation that became a book. On the other hand, it's very common for scientists to publish articles based on their results, often before completing the dissertation.)

• Does the dissertation have the kind of wholeness (that is, coherence and a clear progression from beginning to end) that a book has, or does it come apart into chapters that would more easily lend themselves to discrete articles?

• Were the chapters originally written as separate essays or presentations?

• Do your advisor and other committee members recommend that you publish?

• If you're really undecided, are you willing to try running a book proposal past a publisher?

Publishing Your Dissertation as Articles

You may already have submitted some chapters of your thesis to journals for publication. But if you haven't, and you have decided that you either can't or don't want to turn your magnum opus into a book, then transforming chapters, or portions of chapters, or results of experiments into publishable articles can be a reasonable and more manageable way to get a wider audience for your ideas, and to begin to build your academic résumé.

About timing: start cannibalizing the thesis as soon as you can, before you're totally caught up in a new job, before it seems a bit old and you no longer feel familiar with the material. If you're planning on being an academic, drawing on your dissertation to create articles is a good way to get a jump on one of the most important post-thesis tasks, getting your work published. Ask your committee for advice about how to get published.

How do you choose where to submit your manuscript? Think about the journals that have interested and educated you, consider the kinds of readers that you want for your work and where you're likely to find them, and, once again, seek advice

from mentors. Your advisor and other people who have more experience than you in your field can tell you which journals are good places to send your work, and how to approach them. Spend some time in a university library that has journals in your subject (don't forget that reference librarians are wonderful resources for such information), or browse the Web, looking over possibilities. I send my writing only to journals or magazines that publish authors I respect and enjoy reading; that is, I choose on the basis of the company I'll be in if my work is accepted.

Here are some more issues to consider in choosing a journal:

- Readership/audience. Whom are you trying to reach?
- Editorial policy. Do they take your kind of work?
- Visibility and ease of access. Does your university's library get this journal?
- Turnaround time. Some journals take months, others years, to review submissions. Do you need to have your paper published before a job search or a tenure review?
- If your paper includes figures, photographs, or color illustrations, is the journal known for high-quality reproduction of such material?
- Publication costs. Many academic journals, particularly in the sciences, charge their authors publication costs, but charges are sometimes waived if you're on a grant, or if you or your advisor can negotiate with the editor.
- What is the reputation of this journal vis-à-vis its dealings with its authors?
- What are the length requirements for papers submitted to the journal?
- What is the professional reputation of the journal? That is,

how prestigious is it? What is its acceptance rate for papers? (Beware of new, trendy journals, which may have a good acceptance rate but may not be cited by indexing services or read by the people in your field whom you want to read your work.)

• Who is on the editorial board of the journal, and who reviews for it?

Submit your work to only one journal at a time, unless the publication's guidelines specifically say that multiple submissions are acceptable. Expect to wait several months for a reply; have in mind the next publication you're going to send your manuscript out to, should it be rejected, because no matter how good a piece of work you send off, the odds are that it will be rejected. Prestigious journals in many academic fields have very low acceptance rates.

Should you apply to the prestigious journals? It depends. Some academic departments will not take seriously publication in any other periodicals. But if being in print is more important to you than racking up résumé points, look around at journals you like and find interesting, and try sending your work there. If your manuscript is rejected by the number two journal in your field, don't despair, and still consider sending it to number one. (Every essay I've ever published ultimately appeared in a higher-ranked journal than those that had turned it down earlier.) In fact, consider sending it to number one first. Editors at both book publishing houses and journals are often idiosyncratic. They operate under many constraints: too many submissions and not enough time for screening them, their own particular taste, their appraisal of how your work will fit with other work planned for the same issue, or, for book editors, with projects on their publication list. In addition, trade journals and books are, increasingly in these days of publishing as big business, focused on marketability.

Transforming Your Dissertation into a Book

If you decide that you're going to try to publish your whole dissertation, how do you go about doing it, and finding an appropriate press? Particular presses often specialize in several subjects, and you can discover which publish in your field by noting the titles listed in their catalogs, browsing the library shelves, and, once again, by asking your advisor. You can also look up publishers by subject matter in *Literary Marketplace*, the bible on publishing companies. You'll also have to decide if you're going to send your work to a university press or a trade publisher with a scholarly list. (Basic Books, Pantheon, and Metropolitan/Henry Holt are such trade publishers.) How you answer this question will determine important aspects of how you write your book—such as tone and scholarly apparatus.

Consider some of the differences between a thesis and a book, and the implications of those differences for the work you'll still have to do. Your thesis and your book may differ in purpose, voice, format, and your approach to your audience. You'll want to pay more attention to the style and readability of your book, and to what you hope a less specialized reader will get from reading it.

The purpose of writing a dissertation is to prove to your advisor and your committee that you are capable of carrying out scholarly work at the doctoral level. Most dissertations are written in a formal voice and style and follow a carefully prescribed format that is heavy with scholarly paraphernalia. When you write a thesis, your audience is quite small; the other essential aspect of this audience is that they're obliged to read your work. What you choose to say and, especially, *not* to say in your dissertation is often linked to what you know about your particular audience, and to the fact that they have the power to grant or deny you your degree.

When you turn your dissertation into a book for a wider audience, you can revise your answers to questions such as "What do I really want to do with this, and whom do I want to see it?" How much will you let your own voice emerge, and what do you want the style of the book to be: scholarly, informal, or somewhere in between? Perhaps most important, what is in your dissertation that is worth communicating, and to whom? How will you do so most effectively? You are no longer asking, "Will my committee accept this work and give me a Ph.D.?" You're now asking if your work is marketable.

Look at your book from the perspective of your reading public and ask, "Have I written this book in such a way that readers will keep reading, *even though they don't have to?*" (One friend decided to publish her thesis, a six-hundred-plus-page treatise on torture and censorship in Brazil, after her committee members pronounced it "a good read.") Keeping this question in mind, one of the most important things you need to do right away in transforming your thesis into a book, particularly if you're not submitting it to a university press, is to take out much of the scholarly machinery. But even a colleague who is an editor at a prestigious academic press says, "Tell them to reduce the annotations dramatically and to scotch the lit review."

Your book's opening should be quite different than your dissertation's, which is probably composed of some pretty dense (even if very well-written) theory. What do you want to do with your original first chapter? Do you still want it to be the first thing that meets the reader's eye? You need to convince your book's readers at the outset that it's going to be worth their while to keep reading.

Finding a Publisher and Writing the Book Proposal

How do you choose which publishers to approach about your book? You probably know by now which publishers are most active in your particular field, and which of them have put out the books you think well of. Your advisor or one of your committee members has most likely published one or more books and can be a good source of suggestions, as well as possibly provide you with an introduction to an editor whom she's worked with or whom she knows has a good reputation. Such connections make it more likely that your manuscript will be read, though not necessarily that it will be accepted for publication. It will still stand on its own merits. *Very* occasionally a publisher will approach you; this is a rare occurrence (and if it does happen, it is likely to be a query from a university press). Once again, get advice—from your mentor, but also possibly from a book agent and/or a lawyer—before you sign any contract. (Poets and Writers, Inc., publishes a very useful reference book called *Into Print: Guides to the Writing Life.* Read it.)

Once you've done some library research and some inquiry by word of mouth about publishers, both formally and informally, and have made a tentative list of those publishers you'd like to approach, it's time to write a letter of inquiry. *The Writer's Handbook,* a very useful reference guide for anyone considering being published, remarks in its section on university presses, "Always query first. Do not send any manuscripts until you have been invited to do so by the editor." Write a brief letter that states your interest in having the press look at your proposal, describes your book, and offers a short summary of your credentials ("I have been a graduate student at Superb University for the past five years, two of which I spent in the field in . . . , watching wild rhinos copulate. My master's thesis won the . . . prize for 'most original piece of work on rhinos,' and I have just won a grant from the MacArthur Foundation to return to . . ."). It's also O.K. to summarize your education quickly if you haven't yet accrued such honors. It's very important that the query letter be not only well written but also lively and engaging: you are trying to hook a big fish. It's probably fine to query more than one publisher at a time, because you haven't yet asked anyone to spend any time or energy on your proposal, but seek out the advice of your mentor or a publisher.

Let's say that you receive a letter back from Paragon Press saying that they'd be interested in seeing your work. They may invite you to submit a proposal or a manuscript. The former is more likely. You don't need to have a finished manuscript in order to submit a proposal, particularly since publishers often like to have a hand in the shape of the books they produce. The proposal is a more detailed letter than your inquiry, describing the book and its parts. Work hard at investing this description with the passion you feel for your book; this letter ought to be a persuasive argument for why the publisher will regret it terribly should it choose not to accept your book. You'll be asked to provide an evaluation of the works already out there that will compete with your prospective manuscript; you'll presumably already know some of the competition, but check carefully so you don't end up either embarrassed or having spent a year working on something that's already appeared in someone else's book. Search the various computerized indexes and *Books in Print*, but also go to as many large, academically oriented bookstores as you can to check out what's currently available to readers wanting to learn about the reproductive habits of wild rhinos. (If there aren't any such stores in your town, do some of this checking by phone or via your computer.) Summarize the results of your search in your proposal; it's important for a publisher to know that you've done your homework.

Include along with your proposal your vita, and, ideally, one or a few of your most polished pieces of writing, so that the editor can get some idea of what sort of book you're likely to produce. If you've had an essay accepted by a journal, or if a paper you wrote was well received when you presented it at a conference, consider sending it as a part of your packet. Also offer an estimated date by which you could complete the manuscript for publication. (Don't give yourself a deadline that will force you to work forty-hour days, should the book be accepted.)

Should you try to hire an agent to shop your book around? Not if you're hoping to be published by an academic press. Agents work for a percentage of the money you earn on your book, and most academic presses offer prestige, rather than any substantial amount of money, for publishing your work. The only reason to use an agent is in the unusual case of a dissertation that is likely to have popular audience appeal, and thus will be of interest to a trade publisher. If you think you might, in fact, have such a "crossover" book, it could be worth your while to hire an agent. In exchange for about 15 percent of your earnings, an agent will search for a publisher, negotiate a favorable contract, and absorb the nearly inevitable rejections on the way to an acceptance. Books like Adam Begley's *Literary Agents: A Writer's Guide* (Penguin, 1993) can supply not only a list of literary agencies, but also invaluable advice on finding and working with an agent. An even better way to find a good agent is to ask someone who has employed one whom he recommends highly.

A coda: people have often asked me about hiring outside editors to revise their thesis manuscripts for them. This is a very complicated question. On the one hand, I much prefer to read a book that has been well edited (and there are many books currently out there that clearly haven't been, down to not having been proofread!). On the other hand, editing your book is a job that you should mostly do yourself, with helpful suggestions from literate colleagues and friends—but with you staying in charge of the process.

Rejections

Most of us have one of two (and sometimes both) fantasies about having our work rejected by publishers: either that that's the *only* possibility, or that the first person we send it to will immediately write us back with an acceptance. (There's a third popular fantasy as well: that if the manuscript is rejected, we'll die or never write another word again.) But all of these scenarios are really the exception. The reality of submitting a manuscript is more complicated. If you've polished your work and a mentor thinks it's good enough to be published, it's likely to be accepted eventually, if you persevere and choose carefully both where you send it and how you compose your query letter and proposal. But the acceptance you ultimately receive is not going to come by return mail; you may have to wait several months for a reply by mail or by phone (academic presses are usually staffed by unpaid professional readers with busy work lives of their own). If your manuscript is accepted, you'll often be asked to make further revisions. And, finally, although you may feel awful for a while after you've gotten a rejection letter, in time you can pick yourself up, dust yourself off, and figure out where to send your work next; perhaps before you do so you'll choose to incorporate any useful suggestions supplied by the readers who turned it down.

The best antidote I know for rejection despair is a little book titled *Rotten Rejections, A Literary Companion* (Pushcart Press, 1990), a compendium of awful prior rejections of famous books. For example, this response to *Lady Chatterley's Lover*: "For your own good do not publish this book," or this one, to George Orwell's *Animal Farm*: "It is impossible to sell animal stories in the U.S.A." When I get a manuscript back I also take heart by remembering Madeleine L'Engle's story about her award-winning trilogy that begins with *A Wrinkle in Time*. At the awards ceremony where *A Wrinkle in Time* received the New-bery Medal, L'Engle had a conversation with an editor who had turned down the manuscript for publication (as did several other publishers), who said, "I know I should have published these books."

The Book-Jacket Blurb Exercise

On your way to turning your thesis into a book you will be faced with the problem of how to imagine that thesis-turned-into-a-book, how to envision yourself as the author of something you might one day be able to pick up in a bookstore. Here's an exercise that might help. You have hardbound books in your library, some of them with their dust jackets still intact. Open a few to the inside back flap of the dust jacket and read the author's biography. You'll see that the text there varies widely: some authors are very professional, telling nothing about their private lives; others let a lot, if not all, hang out, down to the names of their pets.

Try writing your own book-jacket bio: write one either for the real book you're hoping to create or for an imaginary one. First write a stodgy, professional one; then try an expressive, hippy version. Experiment with lying: write as if this book won't be your first, but your fourth, and make up the titles and subjects of the first three. Choose the wild hobbies (skydiving, knitting with dog hair, growing exhibition Venus flytraps) you have only in your dreams. Give yourself a pet iguana, or the horse or ferret you've always longed for; six children or none. Have fun imagining the possible author you could be. And then write for yourself what you found out about the kind of writer you wish to become while you were creating your book bio. Doing this exercise may help you get there.

Becoming a Writer

Writing a dissertation is a particularly difficult job because of its powerful symbolic significance, how important it can be in determining your professional future, and how hard it is to write as a novice for the exacting audience of your dissertation committee. You've written simultaneously for yourself and for a very near audience; future writing tasks are likely to be for a more distant one. Now it's time to consider how you feel about writing when you're no longer obliged to do it. Do you have a sense that there might be another book waiting in the wings, material you'd love to take a crack at now that you know how to do it? Will you continue a daily writing habit, and, if so, how will you find the time to do it, when, finally, you are no longer writing a thesis?

Some of you will be pleased to have accomplished your dissertation project, but your heart will now be elsewhere: perhaps in research, with writing up your results as a necessary concomitant task that you now know you're competent to do. Perhaps finishing your dissertation will leave you glad to have done it, but delighted never to have to do anything like it again. Perhaps it will have proved to you that your talents and interests really lie somewhere else. (This last, paradoxically, is an especially good reason to be proud of having managed to accomplish what you have!)

But for others, the experience of writing a dissertation will bring with it an important transformation: it will open up the possibility of being a writer, set you well on the road to becoming one, or turn you into one. But know that even if you want to continue writing, there will still be many days when you'd rather scrub the bathtub. Nevertheless, writing will have become your "practice," as the Buddhists would put it. Perhaps I'm prejudiced in believing you're very lucky if writing has become part of you for life, the craft you now naturally go to in order to think, feel, and clarify problems of all sorts. If writing has become this kind of pursuit for you, you need to make room for it in this next stage of your life. Whether or not writing turns out to be your practice, writing your dissertation will still have changed you for all time.

$\curlywedge$

How the Computer Revolution Affects You and Your Dissertation

BACK IN THE 1970S when I wrote my dissertation, I didn't know anyone who wrote on a computer. We had an early word processor at the Harvard Writing Center, but it took up an entire room! I recall the 1970s to remind you that it is indeed possible to finish a thesis without a computer. For probably less than what a decent computer and printer will cost, you can buy a lot of help (with typing, editing, and hunting down footnotes) from a human being who has access to a computer. If you want a word processor and lack of money is keeping you from owning one, investigate whether your university either loans computers (some even do so free of charge) or has some setup for selling used computers cheap to worthy students. (O.K., so you may not be able to relax in CD-ROM land with your recycled five-year-old model, but that will be one less distraction.) Beware, though, of truly archaic software. Very old word processing programs may not be able to talk to new printers. For example, once you've opened a Word 5.0 file in Word 6.0 and saved it, it may be permanently converted to Word 6.0; if you only have Word 5.0 on your computer, you may not be able to reopen it. Also, make sure that you keep backup copies of your program, not just your document.

The Benefits and Costs of Using a Computer

Computers are wonderful things, and very useful for the large project you've undertaken; the process of revision, in particular, is immensely simplified by them. But computers have costs beyond financial ones. Let's look at some of their uses and some of their costs.

Some people compose directly on the computer; others do their first drafts with pen and paper, and then they type their work into the machine. Composing directly on a keyboard can be a mixed bag: although it can greatly speed up your rate of composition and, in particular, the rate at which your stream of thought gets onto the screen, there are times when the process of writing on a computer is so fast that you don't reflect on what you're writing, so fast that the keyboard directs your thoughts, rather than the other way around. Particularly if you're a quick typist, the temptation is to let your fingers do your writing, and your brain may lag behind. The result is a piece that is more fluent but also more superficial than what you might have written by hand. There are also some of us who find that the presence of a machine in the early stages of composition interferes with our direct involvement with our own words. (Those of you who are thirty-five and younger have grown up sufficiently accustomed to computers so that they do not present this sort of distraction for you; but you may still need to be aware of the possibility of superficiality. On the other hand, a friend of my own age who is also a well-published academic was shocked that I write my first drafts by hand. She writes slowly and carefully on the computer and finds it indispensable for keeping her thoughts and her manuscripts well organized.)

The two opposing viewpoints about composing at the computer demonstrate that you need to think carefully about how the computer works in your own writing process, in order to use its enormous potential as well as you possibly can. There are some people who ought, without question, to compose on the computer: anyone who has trouble with the physical act of handwriting, and anyone who is learning disabled in writing or spelling. If you are in one of these categories, the computer can offer you relief from the tension and anxiety surrounding the physical act of writing itself (in contrast to my tension and anxiety about the possibility that the electricity or hard drive will fail).

Revision is the computer's moment of glory. For most writers the chance to revise with greater ease means it's possible to do more revision, and more revision leads to a better product. And spell checker, grammar checker, and thesaurus features on your computer can really help you along. Revision is where most of the work of writing is. Here the computer allows you to print out all of the pieces of writing you've got, move text around, hack it up, copy it, delete parts and add others, and produce successive versions. You can do the same things without a computer through the judicious use of xeroxes, colored pens, and scissors, and more xeroxes, and lots of scotch tape, but this is a much more complicated way to create drafts. Each time you revise a draft on a computer, copy that draft into another file before you begin to change it, or save each version with a different memorable file name. The original or earlier copy will be essential should you decide that your earlier version of some idea was in fact the better one.

Because of the generation I belong to, and my experience with many dissertation writers, I feel strongly about hard copy. I think it's simpler to see, read, and tinker with drafts if you have them on paper in front of you (it's also easier to mark up your work while maintaining your original text). Even with computers that have large screens, it isn't really possible to see the shape of the document you're composing, or to catch redundancies, or to follow an argument carefully. For this painstaking process, text rolls by too easily on a computer.

For most writers, hard copy of the text feels real in a different way than online text does (particularly since a one-second electrical outage can in fact make an electronic text nonexistent—more about this in the section below on safety). I don't know of any place yet where theses are handed in on disk; as of the publication of *Writing Your Dissertation* you are still writing a book—and it is the growing number of pages that you need to handle, and to feel the weight of. Perhaps some day the number of bytes you produce will give the same psychological effect, but I don't think that's true yet.

Choosing a Computer and Software

Ask people in your department which computers they have used and what they've liked and disliked about them. Take advantage of the computer support services offered by your university and any relevant workshops that are offered. Get the least complicated software that will get the job done. Don't change software, or computers, midstream if you can help it. Check out possible bargains offered by your university on computer prices for new or used machines.

In choosing between a laptop and a stationary computer, you'll have to weigh the trade-offs. With a stationary setup you can get more capacity for less money, if having a portable workplace is not terribly important. With a laptop you'll have a smaller screen and keyboard, and you'll run the risk of losing your machine, or having it stolen, in exchange for being able to work nearly anywhere. (People go to all sorts of lengths to be able to do the latter: a friend who spent a year in a Third World country where the electricity was off eight hours each day spent a lot of her energy finding out how to get the most battery power for the least money.)

Disadvantages of the Computer

If you should happen to be prone to wasting time, the computer is your field of dreams. The dissertation student who used to print out a new copy of her whole opus each time she changed a few lines, and supplied me with scrap paper for life, did, amazingly, manage both to finish her dissertation and to get a good job, but the process took her longer than it should have. I think she was trying each time to persuade herself that she'd done a real revised version, when in fact she'd only pushed a few buttons on the machine and moved stuff around. I've seen other students who got so mesmerized by the technical capacities of their computers that they ended up playing when they should have been working.

There are also other drawbacks to consider:

Mechanical Failures

Assume that sometime in the course of your thesis writing you will have to deal with some kind of mechanical failure, and take precautions accordingly. Hard disks fail, so back up everything you write on floppy disks. Electric power sources surge or get interrupted. Buy yourself a good—not the cheapest—surge protector to plug your machine into, and unplug your computer during thunderstorms. Viruses occur. *Be careful when you borrow software, if ever,* and run a virus-detecting program at the suggested intervals. Most computers can be set up to run virus checks automatically at start-up: it's a good idea.

Losing Files

Back up your files. Back up your files. Back up your files. Floppies are less reliable than hard drives are; you still want to make backup copies using floppies, but if you have access to another hard drive with space, back up there too. If possible, make sure you have personal backup copies of all programs you're using (word processing and graphics). If you can't get at a file because you don't have a program that can read it, you've effectively lost the file, at least until you can find another copy of the program, or a compatible program. In the good old days, I used to put a copy of my dissertation in the freezer, in a waterproof Ziploc bag, before I left my house overnight—in case of fire or burglary. And if you think this was paranoid, I should tell you I learned this trick from a few other thesis writers (maybe it was shared paranoia). Urban legend has it that at least one thesis writer saved his magnum opus from a house fire by having used this strategy. (I also personally knew a scholar whose *single copy of his manuscript* was stolen from his office at a university, in a horrible burglary resembling the one in Dorothy Sayers's *Gaudy Night*.) Keep hard copy, and disks, in more than one place—an easy job with a computer.

Physical Problems

Some at least annoying and at worst incapacitating medical problems can come from working at a computer: neck problems, wrist problems, eye problems. Pay attention to any such symptoms *before they become serious*, and seek expert advice—from computer experts, from your doctor, from a physical therapist. Universities know about these problems. Employee/worker safety offices may be even better resources than the health services. Since they want to help people avoid such ailments, they can advise you about ergonomics and exercises, as well as refer you to the right medical care. Don't let yourself get so incapacitated that you're really unable to work. Better still, find out about the suggested length of work sessions, computer positions, proper chairs, and all such stuff *before* you get started on your thesis.

The Trouble with Formatting

Unless you're a real computer jock, or have thoroughly mastered the details of fonts, footnote production, pagination, and such things, hire someone to do them for you—you will save yourself anxiety, wasted time, and heartache. Get help. Save your strength for the content of your thesis. Footnote organization and formatting details can be an unbelievable time sink. Assume, unless you have good reason to think otherwise, that you're going to get help with this work, and plan ahead by reserving that help.

•   •   •

All of which is to say: Computers are magic. And there is also no such thing as a free lunch.

APPENDIX II

~~~

Some Advice for Advisors

TO THE WRITER: This chapter is for your advisor. Some friends who have supervised many theses suggested that including such a chapter might be one of the most useful things I could do for you. Invite your advisor to read the rest of this book, so the two of you can use it as a starting point for ongoing conversations about how best to work together.

An Advisor's Role

Being a dissertation advisor is, next to being a parent, one of the hardest (and at times the most thankless) jobs around. It calls for knowledge of your discipline, politics, and people; for patience, good timing, a capacity for delayed gratification, and humility. You'll be asked to invest deeply—but not too deeply—in a project that's not your own, for which you'll get no credit. Doing this job is a labor of love, involving what Erik Erikson calls "generativity," the capacity to nurture the next generation. And it won't even get you tenure. (In fact, if you do it for too many people, at the expense of your own scholarship, it may even cost you tenure. My own fine thesis director was a case in point.)

The most important piece of this job is your stance. Being a high-wire trapeze artist is easy compared to the delicacy of what you have to do. What you have to get right—you'll have many opportunities to negotiate this (and to fall off the wire)—is your closeness to and distance from your advisee's thesis project: you need to be close enough to be able to get into its details, but far enough away to make it clear that it's the student's project, not yours.

The appropriate mantra as you approach your advisee is, "Remember who owns this piece of work." If you can stay clear about ownership, many other things will fall into place. For example, you have a heavy responsibility as a reader of the thesis, but none as a writer. You can help or hinder the process, but you can't make it happen. Your responses to the thesis should always be those of a respectful and interested audience. Your job is to advise, to read, to support, and perhaps to nag, but it is not your responsibility whether or not the work gets done. That's your student's choice.

Sometimes you will get to choose your advisee, but more often a student will approach you to ask if you'll advise him on his dissertation. If you don't think you can come to like and respect the person who's asking you, don't take him on as an advisee. Years ago a potential supervisor of mine warned me that she had a poor track record advising women; I looked elsewhere and have always felt grateful to her for the warning. If you know that you are not a good teacher for a particular sort of student—that you have trouble, for example, with the ones who are too much like you, or with those who aren't compulsive about their work, or with those who are less or more independent than you find comfortable—or if you find that you're not much help with certain kinds of thesis topics, at the very least be honest about this up front. At the best, you might be able to suggest to the student someone who would be a better choice.

So you have an advisee with whom you're pretty compatible, you've figured out that this is not your dissertation, and you've sworn not to get pulled unwittingly into writing it. What is your role now? You have several possible roles. The most important one is to be company during a process that you yourself may remember as being quite lonely, to be a steady, empathic, and steadying presence, encouraging and optimistic, and available to meet reasonable demands. You are also a coach, kind but firm, negotiating reasonable deadlines, pushing and pulling the student toward them. You will help her to define the thesis topic, suggest paths best taken or ignored, talk with your student about what constitutes an acceptable thesis, and perhaps provide her with examples of a doable one. (Many writers beginning theses have never looked at others in their field; having a few on hand to suggest as examples—not the most brilliant ones you've ever received—will help advisees begin to imagine their own.)

You'll be available for consultation at sticking points, listen carefully, point the advisee back toward things she's said that may help ("You told me last week that you thought that piece of chapter 2 didn't belong where it was. Do you think it might provide the bridge you're looking for here?"). You'll be willing to discuss the large and small details of the writing process ("How much revision do you really want to be doing this early on? Maybe you ought to save it for when it's clearer which of these sections you're keeping, and which you're discarding." Or "Think about the way you've used the passive voice and commas."). And at the proper moment you'll be an early reader, and then a helpful critic. This begins to sound like a description of an impossible job. In a way it is, and you can be sure that none of your good deeds will go unpunished.

Feedback and Ownership

Here are a few methods and some general principles for thinking about offering feedback on your students' writing. It is sometimes a great help to remember what it was like when you were writing your own dissertation—how it felt, what went wrong, what went well—bearing in mind, of course, that different people have different styles of learning, researching, and writing. It may be simpler to work with students who work more the way you do, but you'll be less tempted to confuse the ones who don't with yourself, or to think that you always know how they feel. Your field has probably changed since you wrote your dissertation, and academic writing styles and teacher-student relations have, too. In *Writing Without Teachers,* Peter Elbow describes some ways of envisioning feedback that both you and your advisee might find very helpful.

Even though you are neither your advisee's parent nor his therapist, the odds are good that at some point during the dissertation process you will be the unwitting recipient of what psychologists call "negative transference." That is, you'll be experienced by the student as the big bad wolf, or the wicked witch, and you'll be the target of his sometimes quite potent anger. The best advice I can offer for such an occasion is to remember that it's a developmental stage of the writer. Don't get into it with him unless you really have no choice (for example, he's bad-mouthing you all over town). Work very hard at not taking it personally, because it probably has nothing to do with you and everything to do with your role and with the advisee's personal history. If you can stay unflappable, the chances are good that your student will cool down.

There are, of course, times when an advisee will be justifiably angry with you: you've failed to tell her about an important deadline, or to warn her in advance that you'd be out of the country at a crucial moment in the project, or you've provided feedback that was not only unhelpful but also demoralizing. At such times you ought to hear her out, accept the blame, and apologize. It is quite surprising to hear what students imagine when their advisors are unavailable, don't return messages, or take an inordinate length of time to comment on materials. The most common responses are statements like "She probably thinks I'm stupid," or "He hates my work," or "I can feel her wincing when she answers the phone and it's me." It may be difficult to comprehend that responses such as these come from quite bright people who do good work. Dissertation writers tend to take the sins of their advisors onto themselves, as in this only slightly caricatured statement: "He probably hasn't called me in the two months since I sent him my last chapter because he began reading it and was so disgusted he couldn't go on, and he didn't want to tell me how ghastly my work is." The fundamental principle of dealing with students in the midst of their dissertations is to assume paranoia.

The best dissertation your advisee can write will come from her feeling that she owns her own work. Ownership is a central force in learning to write. The sort of writing one does in creating a dissertation is an important personal possession, but one that it's easy to lose or have taken away. If a thesis writer is made to feel humiliated or stupid, even if the slight is unintentional, it will be easy for her to feel as if she no longer owns her own words. In order for your advisee to experiment with, test, and change her writing, she has to remain attached to it. I say this despite the fact that for many years I believed that the important next step, for my own or my students' writing, was to "get distance from it," that is, disclaim ownership. I've come to believe that such distance is a myth that oversimplifies or belies the relationship between writers and their writing. It's not so hard to see one's own writing at a distance, but it is hard to bring it back into close focus, to take possession of it once again and engage with it with energy.

How do you encourage ownership of writing in your advisee? Most important is to know and believe that the writing belongs to the student, and to act on that basis. How would your actions bear out such a belief? You would listen carefully to what's being said. You would assume that your student is invested in what he's saying. You would ask him what he intended or meant in a passage you found obscure, and not attempt to guess. You would be careful with evaluations and judgments. You would not write all over his paper, but be properly respectful of it. And—this is absolutely essential—you would not write anything on his dissertation draft that you wouldn't feel comfortable saying to his face.

Given all this, how do we handle feedback and our advising role?

• A very important bit of advice: Before you launch into any detailed criticism of whatever writing your student has given you, say something positive, encouraging, and honest about it. Absent such statements, every dissertation writer I've ever worked with (every other sort of writer, too) has assumed his advisor hated his work or thought it was worthless.

• Best not to lay a thought on your advisee's work—and certainly not a pencil or pen—until you clarify with your advisee what kind of feedback would be most useful for her at this particular point in the process. Ask, "What would you like me to read for? What sort of criticism do you think would be most useful for you right now? Some of my students have found it helpful when I've . . ."

• Be extremely careful about how much feedback you give, particularly early on. Resist the urge to hack, slash, and burn your student's prose, or even just to edit, no matter how awful you think it is at this stage. Consider which one or two main issues it would be useful for *this* writer to hear about at *this* particular point in her work: structural questions? a particular knot in the argument? Do not overwhelm the student with detailed stylistic criticism in any draft before the last one. Remember that many thesis writers are paranoid about their work, and walk carefully.

• Timing is everything. Strong criticism that is essential in the next-to-final draft can be devastating if offered on the first draft. The opposite is also true: offering major criticism for the first time when the work is in its final draft can also be catastrophic. At every stage ask, "Where are we now?" Work on your ability to tolerate early chaos without saying very much. Think before you speak.

• Don't get into a tug-of-war with your advisee—with you "attacking" and him "defending" the thesis. Don't let him off the hook by giving him this opportunity to disown his own negative feelings about his work. Your job is to be good company and the best advocate for this project, in the same corner as its writer (except saner).

• Do not get seduced into turning into a sadist by a student who says, after handing you her first draft, "I want you to tell me *everything* you see in it, including *all* the mistakes." Very few students actually want that much feedback, although many think or say they do.

• This is the student's first magnum opus, and part of the job for him is to learn how to solicit and use feedback, as well as to learn how to judge his own work. Don't feel you have to do all the work for him. Give him both feedback and space.

• Different sorts of feedback are appropriate for different stages. On a first draft it might be appropriate to be encouraging of any writing the student has accomplished, and to comment on a few of her ideas. On the second draft you might ask about the shape of the argument: "What do you think you're trying to say here, and how do you think you might support it?" When you're talking with her about later drafts, your focus will become more detailed and more critical (not negative, critical), but at each stage, don't overwhelm the writer with too much advice at once. There is only so much that any writer can hear and accept at a single sitting. Be respectful, ask her what would be most useful to her, what *her* concerns are about the writing (writers often know where the knotty places are in their argument, or where they couldn't say something important clearly). Listen very carefully to her response.

• Watch your tone. If your customary mien is on the glum side, find some way to let the student know this so she doesn't think that her project has just died. Thesis writers are exquisitely tuned to small signals because you do, in fact, hold their professional life and death in your hands.

• If you have really bad news to deliver (for example, "I don't think the argument of this chapter works as it now stands"), do so gently, and help the writer find a bridge to something else that will work. If possible, don't leave him in free fall.

· Once again, hesitate before marking up a student's draft. Think about the possible effects of doing so. Thesis students have a strange propensity to fantasize that the red ink you've put on their draft is blood—not yours, but theirs or the draft's. Don't use red.

· Think hard about how much energy you have for dissertation advising, and don't take on more students than you can handle well. You will not go to advisor heaven if you take on a lot of students, only if they finish, and that will require a fair piece of work from you with each of them. And don't take on so much work that you neglect your own career: if you fail to get tenure, you won't be able to help any students!

· Be very clear about what you're expecting, about deadlines, about how much leeway there is, and about absolute, nonnegotiable requirements.

· About availability: What has stood out most for me in working with many, many thesis students is how much difference it makes to a writer's progress if his advisor is available. Thesis writing is a very lonely and at times frightening experience. How available you are can make each of these feelings much better or much worse. It is hell to write a thesis long-distance from one's advisor. It is also hell if the student has to call half a dozen times before you call back (I've worked with many students whose advisors took weeks or longer to return calls), or if you neglect to submit the papers required by the graduate offices, or if you take months to give feedback on a chapter. If you think you can't promise not to do these things, turn down requests to supervise theses. That, or clean up your act.

• Make it very clear how and when the student can reach you: tell your advisees what hours, which places, which days are, and are not, O.K. You are not on duty twenty-four hours a day, you do not have to be disturbed at your weekend retreat, and you do not have to make house calls (although I've known one superb thesis advisor who does). But you do have to return calls within a few days, as well as give an advisee reasonable notice of your unavailability (in January, for example, you could tell the student, "If you're not done by the fall, know that I'll be on sabbatical in Turkey the following semester, and I'll read stuff that you send me, but the mail is very slow, and the phone lines are dreadful." Or "The submission deadline for a June degree is April 1. I'm going to be away for a week in mid-March, so factor this into your work schedule.") You should also pick up your phone or E-mail messages regularly, or give your advisee another, more reliable way to reach you.

• Be very mindful of competition. You probably didn't get to your current professional position by being uncompetitive, but work consciously at stashing that inclination while you work with your thesis students, because it's not a fair game—you've won before it begins—and it's too easy to make your advisees feel even more inadequate and insecure than they probably do already. Save your competitiveness for your peers. In the sciences it is more common for researchers to work collaboratively; in the best of such arrangements people both learn more and produce more. In any field, creating a group for your dissertation advisees can help defuse competition among them, and between you and them, as well as allowing them to realize that they can be helpful to others, particularly if you're very careful not to compare one with another in public.

• Your obligation to your student doesn't end with the thesis defense. Seeing her through includes the obligation to consult about how to publish part or all of the thesis, to give advice about professional development and the job market, and to provide encouragement even when the job market is bleak. You don't need to promise heaven on earth, or even a job, but you should be hopeful on her behalf and help her explore possibilities and alternative routes, reminding her that she'll have more than one shot at getting a job.

You should use your professional contacts to get her introductions to colleagues elsewhere who might be of help. You will have to write letters of reference in a timely fashion, so she doesn't lose out on a position because her dossier isn't complete. You also ought to tell her honestly if you feel that you can't write a strong letter of recommendation, so that she can look elsewhere for advocates.

• • •

In summary, being a thesis advisor is like being any kind of committed guide—parent, coach, therapist, or teacher. One has to hang in for the duration, be a reliable presence whose own wants get taken care of elsewhere, and endure a certain amount of getting kicked in the shins. I have an embarrassing memory of an interchange with my advisor from the spring when I was finishing my dissertation. She had just told me the second or third draft of my whole project needed some more work, and I stood outside on the Appian Way in Cambridge with her, shouting, "Won't you *ever* be satisfied?" It's very complicated to be both the nurturer and the one who insists that there are standards to be met, something, of course, that the good parent does as well. It's essential to remember how much power you hold in your student's life, not to abuse it, and to think hard about how best to use it on the student's behalf. When being a thesis advisor goes well, it can be immensely gratifying; the pride that you feel as your "offspring" graduate will remind you not only that your hard work was worth it, but also of how privileged you have been to preside over their growth and learning.

Some Useful Books
and Articles

Begley, Adam. *Literary Agents: A Writer's Guide*. New York: Penguin Books, 1993.

Benedict, Helen. "A Writer's First Readers." *New York Times Book Review,* February 6, 1983; reprinted in J. Bolker, *The Writer's Home Companion,* New York: Henry Holt, 1997; hereafter referred to as *TWHC*.

Bernard, Andre, ed. *Rotten Rejections, A Literary Companion*. Wainscott, NY: Pushcart Press, 1990.

Bolker, Joan, ed. *The Writer's Home Companion: An Anthology of the World's Best Writing Advice, from Keats to Kunitz*. New York: Henry Holt, 1997.

———. "A Room of One's Own Is Not Enough." *Tikkun* (November/December 1994); reprinted in Bolker, *TWHC*.

Burack, Sylvia K., ed. *The Writer's Handbook*. Boston: The Writer, Inc., 1997.

The Chicago Manual of Style, 14th ed. Chicago: University of Chicago Press, 1993.

Elbow, Peter. *Writing with Power: Techniques for Mastering the Writing Process*. New York: Oxford University Press, 1981.

Godwin, Gail. "The Watcher at the Gates." *New York Times Book Review,* January 9, 1977; reprinted in Bolker, *TWHC*.

Goldberg, Natalie. "Writing As a Practice." In *Writing Down the Bones: Freeing the Writer Within*. Boston: Shambhala, 1986; reprinted in Bolker, *TWHC*.

Hanh, Thich Nhat. *The Miracle of Mindfulness! A Manual on Meditation*. Boston: Beacon Press, 1976.

Into Print: Guides to the Writing Life. New York: Penguin Books, 1995.

Literary Marketplace. New Providence, NJ: R. R. Bowker, 1997.

Millier, Brett. "Elusive Mastery: The Drafts of Elizabeth Bishop's 'One Art.' " *New England Review* (Winter 1990); reprinted in Bolker, *TWHC*.

Skinner, B. F. "How to Discover What You Have to Say: A Talk to Students." *Behavior Analyst* 4, no. 1 (1981); reprinted in Bolker, *TWHC*.

Tyler, Anne. "Still Just Writing." In *The Writer on Her Work*, Vol. 1, edited by Janet Sternburg. New York: W. W. Norton, 1980; reprinted in Bolker, *TWHC*.

Woolf, Virginia. *A Room of One's Own:* London: Hogarth Press, 1929.

Index

completed writing as best
reward, 97–98
for met deadlines, 75, 76, 77
for writing through blocks,
94–95
roommates, working out living
conditions with, 68
"Room of One's Own Is Not
Enough, A," 10, 89
*Rotton Rejections: A Literary
Companion*, 148
rules versus principles, xv
ruthlessness, cultivating, 68, 84–85

scared writing, *see* writing scared
sciences, theses in the:
advisor, selection of, 20–21
publishing articles based on, 138
similarities with humanities
theses, xvi–xvii
topic selection, 14
unique aspects of, 14
second through final draft: the
revision process, 116–26,
130–31
advisor feedback, *see* advisors,
criticism from
amount of work involved in,
120
audience, writing explicitly for
your, 124
boredom during, 117, 124
categorical revision, 123
checklist of strategies for, 120–22
computer's advantages in,
153–54

goal-setting for, 124
help during, 130–31, 152
imagining yourself as reader in,
118–19
note taking during, 123
organizational concerns,
119–20, 123
perfection, seeking, 122
psychology of, 116–20
purpose of, 118
quitting too soon, 124
rituals to mark transition from
creation to revision, 123
stamina, 124
staying open to change during,
119
truth telling and, 125–26
vulnerability during, 118
without use of computer, 153
secretarial help, 77, 151
self-flagellation, xvii, 37, 97
"selfishness," 78–79, 89
sentence structure:
in first stage of writing, 35
revising, 122
sexual harassment, 30
"Sharing in the Costs of Growth,"
87, 127
"sit there method" for daily
writing, 44–45
Skier, Kenneth, 46
Skinner, B. F., xvi, 44, 74
sleep, 67, 78, 79, 83
Snow, C. P., xvii
social engagements, limiting,
67–68, 84–85